Tandem Living

BY KRISHANA KRAFT

One young woman's high-risk adventure with
Jesus across cultures, through cancer,
and into the mystery of God.

In *Tandem Living*, author Krishana Kraft, invites readers to redefine uncharted crossroads for invitations to a beautiful life of tandem-living with God. Krishana shares how her experiences crossing language, cultural and medical barriers reveal the gift of an ever-present journey with our Heavenly Father. Crafted with vulnerability, openness, and hope, this book is laced with love and penned intention to help readers embrace tandem living. Whether skydiving, pedaling, punching, sitting or resting, when celebrating God's invitation to live in tandem with Him, we are home. Thank you, Krishana, for your proverbial welcome mat to enter a (re)mission-filled, life-changing way of tandem living.
—*Lydia Criss Mays, PhD, Award-winning Author and Founder of See Beautiful*

Krishana's vulnerability on each page is so real that it makes it hard to put the book down! She will challenge you in your walk with Christ. I'm thankful for her faithfulness through her many battles and obedience to share her story.
—*Kelsi Worrell, Olympic US gold medalist in swimming*

Meeting Krishana Kraft on the mission field in Panama over a decade ago was a huge blessing! Her heart for ministry was so evident, and I was delighted years later to have the opportunity to cheer her on through my B.L.A.S.T. Mentorship Program for aspiring writers and speakers. I know this book is the result of many years of living REAL LIFE and living it WELL —embracing the thrills of victory and the agonies of defeat like a champion. Let her words inspire YOU toward abundant living as well!
—*Shannon Ethridge, M.A./Relationship Coach, International Speaker, and Author of 22 books including the million-copy best-selling Every Woman's Battle series*

Some of life's most precious moments have happened sitting across from a dear friend in a quiet corner of a coffee shop. These pages contain that experience in book form. *Tandem Living* is both heartwarming and heart-wrenching as your friend Krishana sits across the pages and tells you about her journey with Jesus—the rambling yet God-directed adventure through missionary school, Austria, and cancer. Uplifting and beautiful, you'll leave this book like you leave the coffeehouse with your friend—richer because of it.
—*Laurin Greco, Author of* Discover God's Heart *and* The Great Rescue

Tandem Living is a story for people who have faced loss and crisis, for those who have wondered about God's purpose for them, and for those who have wrestled with serious doubts about God and His love. In short, it's a story for any of us. Krishana Kraft comes to us with humor, heart, and deep honesty. *Tandem Living* is a memoir brimming with faith, hope, and love.
—*S.J. Dahlman, Professor of Communications, Milligan College*

Krishana Kraft takes us on an international journey that goes deeper than simply crossing borders. She packs this book—a suitcase—with a dark personal struggle, a deeper understanding of God, and an amazing treasure-trove of people's stories from other cultures. Krishana's genuine candor prepares the reader to venture openly into his/her curiosities, while joining her on her intimate ride with Jesus. Prepare for an emotional yet beautiful ride with tears and laughter at her treasure-finding outlook. This book is a gem, and a must-read for anyone going through—or having gone through—the depths of hardship, be it cancer or otherwise, because it's a travel-guide to discovering God's real presence and true love in the midst of the "yuck" and the good in life.
—*Taylor Beisler, Author / Blogger*

Krishana Kraft is a gifted writer. Journey with her through chapters that will take your breath away with big questions. You will cry and laugh. And in this real-life narrative, you will learn the secrets to finding hope in emptiness, to walking in faith through dark days, to discovering more about the God who never leaves us nor forsakes us.
—*Ruth Schenk, Longtime Contributor,* The Southeast Outlook

Every step we take in life prepares us for the next, and nowhere is that more visible than in this book. Krishana chronicles her life in tandem with God, and how trusting Him for steps in the past help you trust Him for bigger leaps in the future. Krishana Kraft also paints a beautiful, honest, and challenging picture of what it means to be in sync with God—not just pedaling off on an assigned mission.

—Tim Walker, Lead Editor at Orange / Author / Blogger

Tandem Living will take you on an adventure ride which veers off the smooth path, yet will never leave you traveling alone. Krishana's authentic story reveals her heart; a heart which is passionately in love with Christ, and also a heart which must decide how to respond to deep, unexpected wounds. Krishana bravely shares with her readers a brutal honesty with God, and in doing so, invites us to evaluate our relationship with the One who promises to journey with us as well. Krishana's story shouts a richness that is only found in darkness.

—Colleen McKain, Author of It's His Show

Within these pages, I came face to face with the God who is intricately and intimately involved in the tiniest details of my life. This book will awaken your desire to know the Jesus who is longing to listen to your cries, carry your heavy loads, and sit with you in your doubts. I am convinced your heart will resonate deeply with Krishana's story, as she walks through deep pain, asking the hard questions and wrestling with God's mysterious plans. Her vulnerability will open you up to discover the wild adventure you were created to live with Him.

—Charissa Steyn, Creator and Writer at Art of Adventure Blog & Shop

Krishana Kraft's powerful personal story, *Tandem Living*, is replete with honest expressions joy, fear, disappointment, suffering and, ultimately, trust in the Sovereign, Good God. As an instructor at the missionary training program she was attending when she first received her cancer diagnosis, I had journeyed with her from the beginning. We share mutual acquaintances, passions, and a love for serving God in Austria, yet she faced challenges that I have never considered. I have admired her greatly as she stayed focused on her calling from God, with a willingness to trust Him even in the darkest times. Her story will challenge, encourage, and bless all who read it.

—Dianne Collard, Author of I Choose to Forgive */ Europe Ministries Director A.C.T. International*

I had heard of Krishana long before I met her and even in those early days of struggle, I marveled at her tenacity and courage as dream after dream appeared to be crushed by the cancer that was relentless in its efforts to thwart all the possibilities pent up in her heart. When her mother started attending a cancer care support group I'm apart of, the members would wait breathlessly to hear about the epic journey she had been "allowed" to wage against a mighty foe. We stood unseen, and in prayer we lifted her hands, metaphorically willing, pleading that the Lord would grant her stamina and peace in the battle.

I'm so honored to tell you that through reading *Tandem Living*, I have discovered the secret behind Krishana's victory as she traversed the valley of the shadows—it is her unwillingness to doubt that her God, her Lord, would abandon her. Oh, she toyed with doubt, don't get me wrong, but she never gave up on the promises spoken through His Word, nor the faithfulness of the One who gave His life that she might live abundantly.

Tandem Living is written beautifully. It does not fail to bring the reader into the grit and grime and ugliness of cancer. But hovering over every word is grace, mercy, and joy for the road less traveled.

—Judy Gerdis, Author of Get in the Boat! */ Speaker*

I love Krishana's story—the way she shares her life with her readers. *Tandem Living* pulls you in and inspires you to walk boldly with Christ and the people He brings into your life. We can all gain from her adventure—doubt to faith, surrender to GRACE.

—Dave Stone, Pastor, Southeast Christian Church

All Scripture quotations, unless otherwise indicated, are taken from the Holy Bible, New International Version®. NIV®. Copyright © 1973, 1978, 1984 by International Bible Society. Used by permission of Zondervan. All rights reserved.

Scripture quotations are taken from the Holy Bible, New Living Translation, copyright ©1996, 2004, 2007, 2013, 2015 by Tyndale House Foundation. Used by permission of Tyndale House Publishers, Inc., Carol Stream, Illinois 60188. All rights reserved.

Library of Congress Control Number: 2017905367
Krishana Kraft, Charlestown, IN

ISBN 978-0-9987447-9-7

Cover design: Sally Dunn
Cover illustration: Lynn Wohland
Interior design: Sally Dunn

Dedication

For Patricia Louise Kraft, who I remember as "Pat" and "Gran."
You knew what it felt like to face and fight cancer, and I deeply
wish that you could be here for this moment and so many moments
through my story. You also knew what it meant to embrace the
"beautiful view" here on Earth in the midst of difficulty. Thank you
for creating "beautiful view" moments for me, as a child and teen,
that I'll never forget. It's no wonder my first word was "pretty"
while wearing your beaded jewelry. I can only imagine the beauty
you're experiencing now with Jesus.
I love you and miss you.

Table of Contents

Introduction

Foreword

Her laugh is contagious. And magnetic. It simply draws people to her.

And when I heard her spontaneous laughter, I looked up from my desk inside Focus on the Family's *Brio*land to see Krishana Kraft smiling from ear to ear. "I'm your intern!" she announced. As I drew her in for a hug, I knew there was something special about her; something that would last far beyond a one-semester internship. I had the feeling I was connecting with someone for life.

Krishana did a great job with her internship. But it wasn't simply the mechanics she aced. It was her zest for life and her genuine love for people that lodged inside my heart. When we had an opening a year later, I didn't have to think twice about calling her to come back for a fulltime position. Krish loved every minute of journalistic ministry.

She wrote with passion.

She dreamed with vision.

She helped us execute cutting-edge mission trips.

She embraced our audience of 200,000 teen girls as though they were her own little sisses.

It was with sadness and excitement that I watched her leave our magazine staff and head to Austria. I knew she'd hit international soil running at full speed, but I also knew she'd leave a tremendous void in our office. There's really only one speed that Krish knows: Full on.

As you dive inside her story, you'll feel yourself running full-speed together at her invitation. And just as you're understanding the fast paced rhythm that defines Krishana, you'll be forced to slow down. It's then you'll understand the battle fought as she involuntarily decelerated her stride to the demands of her body.

Have you experienced disappointment?

Maybe you know what it's like to dream big . . . and then mourn the casualty of watching your dream file itself "on hold."

You can relate to Krishana's story.

But the story doesn't end "on hold" because Krishana knows the reality of a giant God.

She walks hand-in-hand with the Great I AM so closely that she feels His hand . . . gently pushing,

advancing,

propelling her forward

one faith step at a time.

You'll meet the Great I Am inside these pages. And He wants to do the same for you. He's a master at breathing life into everything that has temporarily filed itself "on hold." Read it and grow. Then give it away and share the miracle.

—Dr. Susie Shellenberger, fulltime speaker and author;
creator of Brio *magazine and editor for nearly 20 years.*

Introduction

For the LORD your God is living among you. He is a mighty savior. He will take delight in you with gladness. With his love, he will calm all your fears. He will rejoice over you with joyful songs (Zephaniah 3:17 NLT).

The water was running in the kitchen, and my mom stood at the counter as she prepared the dishes to go into the dishwasher. I was four and still adjusting to not getting all of the attention since my little brother showed up.

I decided to be the after-breakfast entertainment, singing at the top of my lungs while skipping from the kitchen to the living room to the foyer and back.

"Jesus..."

"This..."

"For..."

"So..."

"Belong..."

"Yes..."

"Loves me..."

"Yes, Jesus..."

"For the Bible tells me so."

My mom tried to figure out what I was singing, but she could only catch the words that I sung in the kitchen before I skipped to the next room. We were living in Olathe, Kansas, at the time, and my entire family had begun to regularly attend church. But my mom had never heard this "Jesus Loves Me" song, which I learned at a Mother's Day Out Program. Something about the truth in those children's song lyrics awoke a curiosity in her heart and mine.

About a year later, both of my parents said yes to Jesus. I watched as their lives and priorities changed. Two years after their commitment, Jesus became more to me than a song lyric. At age seven, I knelt beside my bed, and my parents prayed with me as I asked Jesus to be my Savior. I chose to be baptized and wanted to follow the One whose tune seemed to be composed on my heart. It seemed God and I had met long before I finally decided I'd go where He led. I wonder when He started pursuing me.

As a teen, my commitment to Him grew deeper. I owned it. This was *my* relationship with Him. He loved *me*. Although at the time, I didn't fully grasp what His love meant, how much trust this journey with Him would require, and where this ride would lead.

CHAPTER 1

Giving up

He will feed his flock like a shepherd. He will carry the lambs in his arms,

holding them close to his heart (Isaiah 40:11 NLT).

I sat in the sterile examination room waiting for another mononucleosis test. The nurse practitioner came in and began to examine me. She also noticed the swollen lymph nodes on the side of my neck. Lymph nodes I had noticed for almost a month. They were huge, almost like a large beaded necklace under my skin on both sides. She checked my body for other spots of that nature and asked me a lot of questions. After a few minutes, she asked if she could bring the doctor in. I agreed but was frustrated that I couldn't get a simple blood test and be on my way.

I felt awful. I had already visited one doctor trying to figure out what was happening to my body. He told me I probably had mono, but the mono test came back negative. The doctor encouraged me to get tested again in a few weeks since sometimes mono tests come back negative the first time. This was the only day during missionary training school when I had enough time to go to the doctor because it was Research Paper Day.

I was supposed to work on a research paper about Austria, the country I would move to in a few months to serve on a team with Greater Europe Mission (GEM), that is, as long as the rest of my monthly support came in. Three years ago, I had started this journey. GEM told me from the beginning that support raising would be tough, but it was also taking so long. *God, did I hear You correctly?*

Now here I was in the middle of nowhere, in North Carolina, at missionary training school. Progress! I wanted to make the most of this urgent care outing, so I picked a location about an hour away from the school that included a Panera Bread, Target, Chick-fil-A, and a Starbucks. I guess in a way I was homesick for suburbia or at least something that felt like home.

After driving an hour from the campus, my energy was already spent. I got lost trying to find the urgent care center. After finally making it there, I was both frazzled and stressed. I wanted to be finished with this part of my day. I had a paper to write. I wanted to go to Target. I wanted chicken nuggets and waffle fries.

The doctor came in and examined me. He then told me how large my spleen was by showing me how far it stretched across my body, pointing all the way to the middle of my back. This didn't alarm me because in a mono situation, the spleen is enlarged. But then he felt under my arms and noticed more swollen lymph nodes. "We'd like to do a biopsy," he said. I froze with the sound of that word. *Biopsy.* Questions circled in my head. *Did I even know what that meant? Is that like surgery?*

The doctor mentioned that it could be an infection or it could be something more serious like a type of lymphoma. I was *so* done being in that white, boring, and now scary room. I told the staff at the urgent care that I would need to discuss next steps with my parents. *Tell my parents? How do I tell my parents I need a biopsy when they're eight hours away in Indiana?*

All of a sudden I felt very alone. I left the urgent care center and went to Target. I felt like I was on some kind of survivor's shopping spree. I spent a lot of money buying easy-to-make items, Theraflu, and several DVDs. I would sleep this thing off. Rest really should be the answer instead of a biopsy, and I wanted enough entertainment so I could stay in bed. I rarely got sick or went to the doctor. And I was a long-distance runner (my exercise of choice, so I could eat the high-calorie foods I loved so much, such as pizza). So how did I end up at the doctor two times in less than a month?

As I drove back to school, I could barely eat my Chick-fil-A nuggets. I swallowed hard as I said the word *biopsy* out loud. The sun was setting around the North Carolina mountains. I had to call my parents. The phone rang as I drove with one hand down I-40.

"Hi, Mom."

"Hi. How are you feeling? Did you go to the doctor today?"

"Yes, they did another blood test. But they also did a physical examination. They found more swollen lymph nodes and said they want to do a biopsy."

I couldn't choke back the tears any longer. I heard crying on the other end of the line. I imagined this would affect more than my research paper on Austria. So many details were swimming in my head, so my mom and I said we'd talk more tomorrow. My body was exhausted.

IN THE SHADOW

Since it was February, by the time I got back to the school campus, it was dark. Even my apartment smelled of darkness—damp and cold. There wasn't a roommate to greet me or ask how my day had gone. The medical information I held also felt dark and heavy. I took my Target bags inside and unpacked everything.

I can hold this together, I can! I had been in crazier situations, such as going on back-to-back missions trips to developing countries or moving myself across the U.S. to take a job where I didn't know anyone. Later, I had even quit my job to live in Europe for six months. I knew I had what it took to survive stressful situations. *Come on, Krishana, it's going to be OK. This is probably nothing.* I kept trying to reason myself out of the darkness. I wanted to go to bed, but something told me I needed to share this experience with someone who wasn't miles away. I didn't need to be alone. The longing for warmth and light took priority. So I slowly made my way up to the apartment above me.

I knocked on the door and could see Krista, a tall brunette with shoulder-length hair, get up from her place at the kitchen table. She was one of a handful of single women at this session of missionary training. Her plans involved moving to Sweden. We both enjoyed running, and the few moments when I had enough energy to interact with other participants, she had told me about an upcoming local race. *If only I wasn't so sick.* I wanted to join her for the race, but the condition of my spleen wouldn't allow me to train. I hated being sick. I was missing out on building relationships with other future missionaries, such as Krista.

Throughout missionary training school, I kept thinking, *If only you knew me when I felt better. I really am a fun person. I like to spend time with people and have great conversations.* In a way, I was sad because I hadn't even been able to be myself. I'm usually an introvert who acts like an extrovert. I love to be with people even though I need time to recharge afterward. But my energy level was so low that I barely had enough to attend class and complete my homework.

Most nights I found my bed by eight p.m. Yet I rarely slept through the night. Some nights I'd wake up completely soaked. Then the pendulum would swing, and my sweaty body would be cold. I'd bundle up and hope that the wireless signal would be strong enough so I could watch Netflix to help pass the middle-of-the-night hours when I couldn't go back to sleep. The same was true that night after the doctor's appointment. I hardly slept.

Krista invited me inside. It's hard to be vulnerable with people I desperately wanted to know more, yet didn't have the energy to get to know. I'm not much for small talk, but I tried.

"How's your research paper coming on Sweden?" I asked. I had to find a bridge to admit why I was really there, what I really needed.

She shared what she had found—and thankfully reciprocated the question.

"I didn't work on my paper today. I used the time to go back to the doctor," I explained. I shared about the mono suspicions I had before I came to North Carolina and the need to get a new blood test. I told her about going to the urgent care center and what the doctor had said about a biopsy. Telling her what had happened felt like I had taken off a heavy backpack. She hugged me and prayed with me. God knew I needed to bring someone else into my unknown. Into my fears.

How can I leave missionary training school? This has been what I've been working toward for almost three years. I pictured the stacks and stacks of envelopes

I had mailed to raise monthly financial support. There had been countless breakfasts, lunches, and dinners I hosted where I barely ate because I was focused on sharing my heart for Austria and inviting others to support me on this journey.

This wasn't the first time I had set toward a goal, sometimes out of sheer determination. I came from a long line of perseverers and performers, acquired from my mom who also loved making lists, planning adventures, and creating function out of chaos. I learned how to perform well from her; she learned it from her dad; and he learned it from his mom. Give us a goal and we'd get there, while seeking to perfect the end-result along the way.

Even at age three, I had the perfect performance ready for whenever guests would come to our home. I couldn't read, but would hold the book *The Three Little Pigs* and recite the story from memory, coordinating my words with the pictures on each page.

Now, I was proud of the independent, single woman I had become. I could move anywhere, find community, and create a life there. I could be financially responsible and had even managed to raise seventy-five percent of the funds I needed to move to Vienna. And my new German language skills were good enough to order coffee and even make my way through big cities on public transportation.

My tendency wasn't just to persevere or perform, but doing it in such a way that it couldn't fail. Being one step ahead of what might cause failure. Now, here I was face to face with my enemy—failure. And I couldn't perform my way out of this. I desperately wanted to finish this training so I could finally get to where I wanted to go all along, Vienna, Austria.

After recently spending time in Austria, I emailed Dawn, one of my future teammates living in Vienna, to tell her what was happening with my health. Dawn and I first met a year ago standing in the cold early morning hours outside of a Vienna government office. It was January, the dreariest month in Austria, and we were waiting for the building to open so we could apply for our resident permits—allowing us to live in the country for more than three months at a time.

She and her husband, Joel, and two teen daughters had only lived in Vienna for a short while. I could tell she wasn't a morning person. She kept quiet in sharp contrast to Joel and our GEM-Austria director, Jim, who struck up a conversation. I consider myself a mid-morning person, although I can't imagine any morning person enjoying the five a.m. January cold, even if you are in a beautiful city like Vienna.

One night during my five weeks in Austria, Dawn and her family invited me for dinner. It was easy to talk to her, almost as if we had known each other for a long time. I asked tons of questions about living in Austria and how they decided what to bring with them. Dawn and her family had a rental house instead of an apartment, which wasn't typical. However, she showed me around and told me about the furniture they packed and the items that helped their space feel like home in a foreign country. Before I knew it we had spent three hours talking after dinner. Those conversations began a friendship.

Dawn had previously been an oncology nurse. So when I got the news about a biopsy, I told her about my symptoms. She told me I needed to take care of my body, that I couldn't flunk missionary training school, and that I could always finish the paper later. It was like she gave me permission to prioritize my health. I wasn't getting better, and I needed the right support system around me.

I couldn't maintain the schedule and required stamina any longer.

After a few days of working out details, I decided I would need to leave school and head back home to find out what was going on with my body. My dad would fly into the Charlotte airport, and then we would drive back together. Until then, though, I still didn't stop. This isn't what I had imagined my missionary training school experience to be. So I wanted to do whatever I could to say I had finished strong. I imagined this training school as a marathon, much like the one I ran in Chicago six years before. You don't quit even when you feel like it. When you "hit the wall," you dig deep and keep going. I know God sustained me, but I was also determined.

As I lay awake the nights before my dad arrived, I sensed God whispering Isaiah 41:10 over me, "So do not fear, for I am with you; do not be dismayed, for I am your God. I will strengthen you and help you; I will uphold you with my righteous right hand." I didn't know how this would impact my plans for moving to Austria or raising support for missionary work.

NO MORE STRENGTH

Six days after that urgent care appointment, my dad was on his way to help me pack my stuff and drive me home to Indiana. His laid-back personality and dad-jokes greeted me as he slid into the passenger seat of my car. He immediately offered to drive, but I could push through one more hour.

After lunch, I handed him the keys. I didn't have to force myself to keep going. I had been so sick yet continued to write papers, while making sure I had enough fluids and food. I was so thankful that my dad was there to pack my car for the journey home. Packing my car should not be a difficult task, but I couldn't be strong any longer. I finally let someone take care of me. Once we were packed, my dad and I went around to every apartment to say good-bye.

We got on the road the next morning. And I didn't know where this journey would lead. What would happen to this dream of living in Vienna? I felt so strongly that God had brought me this far. Hadn't a three-year delay in gathering financial support been enough of a detour? Where were we headed now?

CHAPTER 2

Will You Join Me?

But those who trust the LORD will find new strength.
They will soar high on wings like eagles. They will run and not grow weary.
They will walk and not faint (Isaiah 40:31 NLT).

Three years before

I parked my car and climbed into Lauren's vehicle. As I took my seat, someone asked if I was nervous. I was—for many reasons. They had no idea about the events that had just taken place while I was at work, but they knew where we were headed. My stomach had been in knots all morning, and we still had a two-hour drive to Longmont, Colorado. With two cars in tow, the group headed north to celebrate Lauren's eighteenth birthday. The destination: tandem skydiving.

I had met Lauren and her family at church in Colorado Springs, Colorado, where I was her high school small group leader. Her fascination with skydiving began at age fourteen when her dad took the 98 FTS Commander's position for the parachute training and demo squadron at the Air Force Academy.

Lauren is the kind of person who likes to know *all* of the details before she does something. For skydiving, she made sure she knew about the safety and statistics. You might think researching tandem skydiving would only deter a person from actually doing it. However, for Lauren, the statistics she discovered made this quite safe in her book.

She had watched her dad jump and heard about him training Air Force cadets to jump. Now it was her turn, and she was pumped! She even planned for two of her friends to join us. How I got involved with this birthday adventure is beyond me, but I do remember telling people it had something to do with being a great small group leader. Doesn't every high school small group leader join her students for tandem skydiving when they turn eighteen?

I love celebrating birthdays, so it was only natural to make a big deal about it. Typically, the birthday girl from our group would be at home getting ready for school when I'd organize the rest of the group to show up in her living room ready to take her out for breakfast before school. Whenever we were on a surprise birthday mission, Lauren would always remark, "We can sleep when we're old." I agreed. There were too many moments of life I didn't want to miss because I was sleeping.

When we arrived in Longmont, we had to sign a handful of papers. *Here I go, literally signing my life away.* Then the instructors led us to the blue jumpsuits and goggles. *Am I really doing this? What happens if I die? Oh, I can't let my mind go there.* Lauren's dad explained what to expect and what it felt like to jump out of a plane; we wouldn't feel that stomach-in-your-throat feeling. I doubted his words would be enough preparation for the jump I was about to take.

Then I met my tandem-skydiving instructor. I wanted to start firing questions at this twentysomething guy, but he distracted my thoughts with the timeline and instructions on how to exit the plane. *Exit the plane! What if I forget what to do?* He asked if I wanted to pull the parachute. I refused. I didn't want *any* responsibility. Remembering to count to three before exiting the plane was enough!

After Lauren, her friends, and I received our instructions, all of our instructors led us to the plane. This was probably the smallest plane I had ever been on. I wonder now if not having air-conditioning on board is necessary to get all those jumpers to jump. In a small plane with about fourteen other people, it warmed up quickly and all I wanted to do was get out of the plane as fast as I could, longing for fresh air. We straddled long benches, each of us with our tandem instructor sitting behind us. Each instructor connected his harness to the harness of his jumper. While the final preparations were underway, my videographer, who planned to capture the entire moment on camera, asked me important questions such as, "Do you trust that guy sitting behind you? Do you have any words of wisdom before you jump?" *Now I'm really crazy! I only met him fifteen minutes ago and now we're jumping out of an airplane.* All I could think to say was, "Happy Birthday, Lauren!"

At 17,500 feet above Longmont, they opened the door and my instructor reiterated the instructions he gave to me on the ground. *Oh dear!* We crouched down at the door of the plane. "On the count of three, we are going to rock ourselves out of the plane." 1, 2, 3! All of a sudden I went from squatting to flying. Well, I was actually *falling* at 120 mph, but it sure didn't feel like it.

Before I jumped, the videographer told me to grab his hand when we saw him. I had no idea how he would exit the plane right after we did, and yet somehow find us in the middle of the vast sky. Yet, there he was! I focused so much on finding him, grabbing his hand, and smiling for the camera, I forgot I was falling. When I did glance below, the Colorado Rocky Mountains looked so small.

When my tandem-skydiving instructor pulled the 'chute, my entire body jerked upward. Now we were smooth sailing to our final landing destination. I actually did this! I couldn't wait to tell my friends and family—and this jump wasn't the only news I had to share from this wild day.

Earlier that day...

My stomach was already in knots, and I was still five hours from jumping out of an airplane. However, this was going to be my first true jump of the day. I hadn't planned to go into work because of my tandem skydiving excursion, but trying to nail down a time to talk with my boss, Susie, was complicated. Besides being an editor of *Brio* magazine, she also wrote books and spoke at churches and Christian conferences many days out of the year. The day before, I shared my plans with her and we decided to gather the staff for a morning breakfast meeting—donuts! I walked into the conference room in my nonwork attire, jeans, tee, and sneakers instead of a dress, hose, and heels.

Ugh, donuts. I don't think I could eat a donut right now. I wondered if my stomach would feel better once I announced my resignation. *Oh, wait, later on I'm jumping out of an airplane.*

Along with Susie, the four *Brio* staffers filed into the corner conference room. As they walked in, they immediately noticed my jeans and began chattering about my upcoming skydiving, probably thinking Susie had called this meeting at the last minute and asked me to come in. I wondered what my face looked like as each woman glanced toward Susie and then toward me trying to piece together the reason for this impromptu gathering. Could they see my nervousness? Susie thanked everyone for coming and told the group I had an important announcement to share. *Here goes nothing!* I explained a bit of the process God had taken me on and said my last day with *Brio* would be after our annual missions trip in approximately two months.

After holding this information for so long, my shoulders relaxed like after a good massage. I no longer had to carry this news alone. Now, I could ramble freely about my excitement for what was next. I glanced around the table. It seemed no one knew what to say. So they followed Susie's lead, "We're going to miss you, Krishie, but we're excited for you." With sad faces, they slowly made their way toward me for a hug.

I had been a college intern with *Brio* and, in a way, grew up during my time on staff. I had laughed, cried, and traveled the world with these women. They were more than co-workers; they had become like family.

I looked at the time and realized I needed to go. As I pulled away from the office, I knew things wouldn't be the same the next time I went to work. *I can't believe I officially resigned from my job. God, this feels absolutely insane.*

I WANNA GO

More than a year before jumping out of an airplane, I told my boss, Susie, I wanted to quit my job and move overseas. I wasn't sure what that looked like, but it didn't matter because I was not sure she believed me anyway. I was the associate editor for a Christian magazine for teen girls published by Focus on the Family (Focus) in Colorado Springs. It was my dream job. I was able to combine my love for writing, editing, youth culture, and my relationship with Jesus in this one position—and I got paid for it. Susie constantly thought of unique ways we'd connect with our readers, to the extent that we joined anywhere from 500 to 1,000 of them on annual mission trips to Central or South America. Writing, traveling the world, and helping teen girls navigate life and build strong relationships with Christ—*what more could I ask for?*

Then one day I sat in a room with publishers from around the world. We handed out magazines. These publishers visited Focus hoping to find out how they could produce quality publications with a Christ-centered message in their own countries. One of the publishers raised his hand and asked when Focus would come to his country and create teen resources of this caliber. The room grew silent, and all eyes stared at the staff in charge of the meeting.

The gentleman went on to explain he wanted someone to come to his country, study his culture, understand the issues their teens faced, and discover how to reach them. With each of his words, my heart responded with, *Yes!* God gave me these gifts, abilities, and passions to create through the written word and use them to draw teens closer to Jesus. I needed to use them to reach teens in another part of the world. As Susie and I walked back toward our desks, I felt like I had just attended a pep rally for my heart. If I had known where to go or what to do next, I would've packed my cubicle immediately and headed out of town. God had my attention.

God, are You speaking to me? Do You want me to leave my job? Do You desire for me to leave the comfort and security of living in the U.S., earning a regular paycheck, being close to family and friends? I was willing to stay *and* willing to go.

JUMPSUIT—CHECK; GOGGLES—CHECK

As I prayed, waited, and watched, God's direction showed up in Scripture, through conversations, and in the way He orchestrated certain circumstances. This is how I heard from Him. The stories in the book of Acts screamed the theme of availability. *How would my availability influence a life?*

As I looked back on the year and where I had been available, I realized that even my role leading a high school small group pointed toward Austria. Sarah, one of those girls, attended a Torchbearers Bible School in Austria after high school graduation. Before leaving, Sarah hinted that I should come for a visit. She could see how my face lit up when I talked about my dreams to travel to Austria someday.

I had been there twice—the first time as a high school student while on a missions trip with my church and my second visit while on a college humanities trip. The beauty of Austria had been etched as postcards on my heart: images of mountains with snow and others with lush green grass and green-leaved trees, and quaint villages nestled in the valley of towering mountains. On Sundays, life stood still in Austria. Shops closed, and Austrians spent time with their families. I longed to visit Sarah there but didn't want to go alone. Her younger sister, a high school junior, Ashley, wanted to go too.

As our trip to Austria approached, I connected with a missionary family living there. They had a remarkable story to share that would make a great article for *Brio,* so I made plans to visit and interview them. Then just before leaving, I attended a Colorado Springs missions fair and talked with someone from Greater Europe Mission (GEM), an organization primarily focused on serving and reaching those in Europe. *Europe and specifically Austria continues to come across my path and in front of my face. God, what do You want me to do with all of these pieces?*

My quick week in Austria left me with a lot to think about. Living overseas as a single woman wouldn't be easy. On the tough days, it could get lonely without a spouse or family to come home to. I wouldn't even have the English language to rely on in calling my landlord, getting around town, or tackling challenges along the way. Regardless, I could always come back to God's faithfulness, right?

When I returned to the U.S., I explored what a six-month sabbatical would look like. *Would there be a way to explore missions and still keep my job? Could I attend a Bible school like Sarah? What could I do to see if Austria was the next step?* Finally, I came across a program in Mödling, Austria, just outside the city of Vienna. This six-month missions training program had a focus on youth outreach. I couldn't find a way to stay at *Brio* and participate in the overseas program. Each little piece led to one more step, almost like God handing me the jumpsuit and goggles, and leading me in the direction of the plane. From my perspective, the only option now was to join Him, leave my job, and take a jump.

The signs pointed to Austria, but I still wrestled with giving up my secure life in Colorado Springs. I had wonderful friends, a nurturing church community, and a stable and fun job. Why would I give up all that for something that only held unknowns?

Four months after I had been accepted into the program in Mödling, I still hadn't told many people, including those on the *Brio* staff. I prayed about when to share the news, and God impressed on my heart that not everything He shares with me ought to be immediately told to the world, a characteristic of any intimate relationship. He would give me the cue, the "1-2-3" before I jumped into that announcement.

A NEW TYPE OF LIVING

I hadn't planned to take two jumps in the same day; it just happened. But I began to think about their similarities.

It seemed insane to connect my skydiving harness to my instructor's harness after only meeting him fifteen minutes before taking off in an airplane. He was the experienced one; whatever he told me to do, I did. He told me when to put on those fashionable goggles and when to crouch down by the airplane door. He also explained when we'd count to three, so I'd put my head back and keep my legs bent so my back would be arched as we exited the plane. If I hadn't been in a tandem connection with my instructor, I would've had the most terrifying fall of my life. Most importantly, I didn't have a parachute, but he did. His experience and guidance landed me back on the ground in one piece.

This picture of trust was a gift. It was almost as if God whispered, *Krishana, I want you to be so closely connected to Me that you move wherever I take you.* For me, tandem living was a picture of what it meant to trust God. It wasn't just a one-time "OK, God, I trust You." This was a type of trust that signaled a deeper relationship. He wanted me to harness myself to Him. To abandon the safety of the plane, to jump when He said jump, and to surrender my life into His hands.

I had no idea how tandem living would grow into its name.

CHAPTER 3

What Do You Really Know?

Now we see things imperfectly, like puzzling reflections in a mirror,
but then we will see everything with perfect clarity. All that I know now
is partial and incomplete, but then I will know everything completely,
just as God now knows me completely (1 Corinthians 13:12 NLT).

I *should be able to answer a question about knowing God, right?* I wanted to retort in a persnickety voice, *Well, of course I know God!* Or at least I thought I did.

"Do you know God?" he had asked.

I wanted to leave the room and cry. I had met this youth leader during a youth event in the summer of 2006 just a few minutes before this conversation. He didn't know me or my story. But something about his question stirred more questions in me. Here I was surrounded by looming change and expectations about what my life should look like as a missionary. I stood there for a moment. I mumbled, "Yes," but hesitated to even say that while teens and youth leaders swirled around me. Immediately, my mind went to another conversation, one I'd had with the missionary I interviewed in Austria. She had emphasized, "If you can't share Christ in your life and in your words in the U.S., then who's to think you'll be able to do it in another country?"

In a month I'd move to Vienna for six months. *What in the world am I doing, God? Do I really know You? Did You really lead me to take this faith jump to Austria?*

My world had been turned upside-down since I announced my plans to leave my job and move to Vienna. Everything was so exciting in the beginning, and I loved new adventures. Then I realized all of this adventure came with an unfamiliar location and culture, it required living far from my community, and this adventure brought all of the self-imposed expectations of being someone who not only knew God, but who also was confident enough to talk about Him to others.

WHERE'S THAT PARACHUTE?

After being awake for almost twenty-four hours, finding a luggage cart in the Vienna airport felt like a nightmare. The machine wouldn't take any foreign currency—only euros. I didn't have a single coin. *Where was I supposed to exchange money in baggage claim? I should've exchanged some money before I left Denver.*

Trying to solve the luggage cart dilemma had me sweating. The two big duffle bags I had packed sure would fit nicely on a cart rather than me trying to carry them both through customs. I had packed clothes for three seasons: fall, winter, and spring—but summer clothes would have been lighter. My backpack weighed at least twenty pounds but felt like fifty under stress. It was probably over the weight limit for most carry-ons, but somehow I managed to get it onboard. I was beginning to relate to the woman who sat next to me during the long, international flight to London. She was terrified of flying, and at one point she had an unrelenting grip on her husband's hand and was breathing into a bag to keep from hyperventilating. *I've only been in Austria for fifteen minutes, and I may need to breathe into a bag.*

I could see the luggage starting to arrive in baggage claim. Desperate times called for desperate prayers. *God, please help me right now! I'm not sure what to do with all of this luggage.*

A short, elderly gentleman, dressed in his Sunday best came up to me while I fumbled with the luggage carts. He handed me a coin and mumbled something in German I didn't understand. I smiled as he talked. Maybe he had found it on the ground or maybe he felt sorry for me. Who knows? I didn't care how the coin appeared, I was grateful.

God, is that You? Or is that happenstance?

Before I knew it, the heavy luggage I had dragged off the baggage-claim conveyor belt was loaded in a car, and the missions program leaders drove me and another student toward the Vienna suburbs. There were only three students—all females—in the program. Courtney, who joined me in the backseat of the vehicle, was a tall, short-haired brunette. This college freshman had traveled from Washington State with a heart for the world and for mentoring girls.

After arriving at a small, yellow A-frame house, our leaders guided us to the bedroom we'd all three share. As the door opened, a short, curly-haired brunette quickly stood up and introduced herself. "Hi, I'm Mallory!" I could tell she had arrived yesterday; she didn't have the jet lag Courtney and I reflected in our tired eyes. Mallory, hailing from the northeast corner of the U.S., had graduated high school and wanted to take a year off before heading into college.

Here I was eight to nine years older than both students. I had already experienced adult life with bills, a job, independence, and responsibility. Would they think of me as a fellow student or as their youth leader?

Everything about Austria was a novelty those first few weeks, from experiencing the Billa (local grocery store) to the weekly topics we discussed in the program. Each week, the theme changed, building on the previous week. The lessons were primarily about God's attributes and our relationship with Him. Instructors traveled to our little house in Mödling to share their stories, experiences, and the Scriptures that had impacted them regarding that weekly topic.

After two months into the course, the intensity increased as we dug deeper into God's attributes. For me, His characteristics of being my Father, felt like a worn blankey. That was the God I ran to—He provided me with comfort, and I was familiar with this side of Him. Or so I thought.

We then approached the topic of the Holy Spirit. I knew the Holy Spirit lived in me from the moment I recognized my need for Jesus and accepted His gift of salvation (Ephesians 1:13-14; Romans 10:9-10). And I knew God's Spirit had led me to this place. Yet, now I rubbed shoulders with people from a different culture, who held perspectives and experiences with God wholly unfamiliar to me.

Courtney, Mallory, and I sat in the small classroom, right off of our bedroom. It was mid-week into our study of the Holy Spirit, and I was uncomfortable. All this talk about God's Spirit didn't fit into my view of God as my Father. A vibrant, middle-aged, husband-wife team were our teachers for the week. They asked for questions as we concluded our morning session on spiritual gifts. These weren't unfamiliar Scriptures to me, but it seemed that the deeper we dug into this topic, the more foreign God felt.

"After lunch, when we meet for our next session, we'll discuss healing and even practice," the wife gleefully added.

"Be thinking if you have something physical that needs healing," her husband chimed in.

If only someone had taken a snapshot of my face. I'm sure my eyes were as big as saucers, and my mouth gaping. *Healing? I didn't know you could schedule those.*

My stomach wasn't hungry for lunch. I tried to nibble on a sandwich, but my mind was focused on the afternoon session.

As we gathered after lunch, the husband-wife team asked for volunteers. *Um God, I want nothing to do with this. No way!* I remained stoic in my seated position, wondering how this would play out.

Finally, one of our leaders volunteered for them to pray for the back pain she suffered. After receiving a handout noting Scriptures about healing, I kept my eyes opened and watched as this husband-wife team prayed boldly for healing. I knew in my head that God had the power to heal, but I wasn't so sure about His timing in this situation. I found it difficult to believe in my heart for this immediate healing.

I tried to join them in the prayer by shutting my eyes to connect with the God who still felt familiar to me. *Was this room getting warm?* My palms were sweaty as I peeked. *God, praying for healing like this feels so manipulative. Is this really part of who You are?* It felt as if this afternoon session would never end. I wanted out!

After the healing prayers ended, our leader admitted she felt some back relief. I had trouble holding that moment alongside the familiarity and comforting attributes I knew of God. Could I integrate every characteristic of God I had experienced with the ones I hadn't? My God-box felt like it was about to implode.

RUNNING IT OUT

I needed to get outside to think. This quaint town backed up to a forest with several hiking paths. Whenever my free time collided with favorable weather, I'd take advantage of a running/hiking/walking adventure on my own. When I lived in Colorado, time alone outside was a way to both process and pray about whatever was bothering me. The ironic thing was that God was bothering me. I needed to talk to Him about His character and all of these pieces of Him I didn't understand.

I put on my running shoes, headed out the front door, down the stairs, and walked toward the woods. Once I arrived at the path, I started to jog. Most of the journey was uphill. The Austrians had walking sticks to help them speed walk up these hills. They looked like skiers equipped with only their poles.

I approached a wooden sign naming towns and trails in the area. Courtney, Mallory, and I had hiked this before and made it to the Mödling Castle ruins. When I'd come out here alone, though, I didn't have a similar experience. I'd forget the route and end up seeing the castle ruins only from a distance. I was hoping today wouldn't be that day.

I took a left and started up and down the hilly path. As I turned the bend, I could see the white stone on the hill. "Yes!" I shouted as I decided to push myself and pick up speed.

After climbing some steps, I worked on slowing my breathing as I stepped into the largest structure, which had five windows facing different views of this area of Austria just south of Vienna. I climbed up into one of the windowsills of the large stone structure and stared out at the trees and the leaves starting to change colors.

Everything *was* about change.

God didn't feel comfortable anymore. Maybe God isn't supposed to ever feel comfortable, but I had gotten comfy with the ways I viewed Him.

God, I come to You as a little girl. I feel so small. I feel so confused. I know in my head You are holy. You are righteous. You are powerful. You have more power than my mind can even comprehend. I don't want to put You in a box. I want to know You for who You really are. I want to know You intimately. Are you still my God?

My heart shouted from that windowsill, while my mouth remained silent. I needed to hear from Him, to know Him. As I climbed down from the windowsill, I picked up the pace and headed back toward the A-frame house. In my room, I noticed a card on my pillow from a friend back home:

"And this is my prayer, that your love may abound more and more in knowledge and depth of insight" (Philippians 1:9).

The words were a balm to my ache.

God, I want my love for You to grow in knowledge and depth of insight, even when I don't understand You. I long for that. Help me to not fear brokenness, but to embrace it. Thank You for meeting me right where I am.

I remembered the "1-2-3." The jump to Austria seemed so obvious. The program I was in appeared to be the next step. But I had so many questions, like all the questions I had for my tandem-skydiving instructor before the jump but didn't have a chance to ask. (I mean, how many times had he jumped out of an airplane? That would've been helpful information.)

As I realized the breadth of my unfamiliarity with God, I wondered why He brought me here. I was all about long-term planning and jumping toward that next action. I thought I was coming to this program to not only work but also to figure out next long-term steps of how I could serve God in Austria. Instead, God desired for me to get to know Him. A God of ways beyond my own (Isaiah 55:8-9).

BIGGER

Not long after our week on the Holy Spirit, our team headed to Kaufering *[Kow-fih-ring]*, Germany, to live in a castle and join another missions training program with students who spoke both English and German. Living in a castle was so appropriate because God had been trying to remind me that I was still His daughter, His princess.

Even when I couldn't wrap my mind around all the pieces of His character, He wanted me to rest. To simply *be* His daughter, instead of working, working, working so hard to figure Him out.

But I'm not good at resting. Yep, I was known for hopping on one plane and then on another, traveling around the world and filling my schedule with many good things and leaving little room for margin. Now, it was time to stop and *be* and to absorb new knowledge of God.

While living in a castle for a week, I met some incredible young women. One of them, Karolin, a redhead from Germany, spoke wonderful English, and we bonded because we were both introverts needing our own space, which in this program was a high commodity.

I eyed Karolin getting her food at lunch. I wanted to snag a few moments with her. "Karolin, can I join you?"

"Of course, Krishana," she smiled. "I will sit over there," she pointed to a table off to the side of the dining hall.

Once we had our food and began eating, I let the question that I was really chewing on be known. "Karolin, do you ever question what you know or think you know about God?"

"Yes," she responded. "At times, this missions training program has taken me outside of my comfort zone."

"Me too," I confessed. *God, how much more out of my comfort zone are You asking me to go? I left my job, I left my country, and now You are not even familiar.*

"We should pray for each other," she suggested.

She was right. We did need to pray. After we finished eating we pushed aside our dishes and joined hands. The dining room had cleared out so we had a few minutes of quiet.

"I'm going to pray in English, but if you want to pray in German, then that works for me. God knows what we're saying even when we don't always understand each other." I said.

"Thank you," she smiled.

It didn't matter that the only German words I could pick out of a conversation were the ones for "please," "thank you," and "power" because in German it was the same as my last name, "Kraft" and showed up in worship songs. Karolin brought me and my struggle before God, the God whom I desired to live in tandem with. She must have prayed about His power and for me to have the courage to simply trust Him. I had little idea of what was being said, but I felt more connected to Karolin in that moment than I had during our entire time together.

It didn't matter that I had kept God in a box or that there was a language barrier. God went beyond all that to help me understand the meaning behind the words Karolin prayed. He is the One who unifies and creates bonds that go beyond words. He bonds hearts through His Spirit.

I started this journey harnessing myself to God. Even though I had known Him much longer than the fifteen minutes I knew my tandem-skydiving instructor, it still felt just as short. Yet I followed Him, and now I felt as though I was just waking up to even a little more of who He is. Could I say I knew God? Well, yes. Was there more to Him than I knew? Definitely.

CHAPTER 4

Guided

You light a lamp for me. The LORD, my God,

lights up my darkness (Psalm 18:28 NLT).

A ten-hour train ride back to Vienna by myself. I couldn't wait. I had extended my time in Germany to visit some friends, and now I needed time alone and personal space to recharge. I needed time with God. He used to feel like home, but now I was homesick in more ways than one.

I grabbed my backpacks and waited for the bus. The bus came right on time, and I guess the driver was feeling generous because he didn't make me pay to ride. I pulled out the full travel itinerary. The sheet listed every train, departure time, and departure platforms in order to make my connections.

My train left at 12:29 and I had an hour to wait at the station, but I kept pulling out the train itinerary, anticipating the next leg of the journey.

Boarded my train to Ulm. OK, one down and four more to go.

While standing at the platform waiting for my second train, I heard an announcement. It might as well have been Charlie Brown's teacher, because I didn't understand any of it. I watched the people around me as their expressions changed. The group started to leave the platform. *What is going on?*

I sat down on the closest bench I could find, pulling my laptop from one of my backpacks. Would Skype work here? No Wi-Fi. And I didn't have a phone. There was no way I could contact anyone who knew me. My heart started beating faster and faster. Tears welled up in my eyes, but I held them back. Gulp. *God, help.*

Nervously, I went into the main terminal. I approached the service desk where a young woman sat helping other customers connect with their final destinations.

"Sprechen Sie Englisch?" I asked, hoping someone would say yes, and bring clarity in English to this situation.

"Yes," she responded.

"I need to get to Mödling, Austria." I handed my train tickets and itinerary to her.

She reviewed the information. "Due to railway construction in Munich, most trains are delayed at least an hour," she replied. After typing some information in her computer, she printed off a new itinerary. I glanced at the schedule and noticed she had added another train to the five I had already planned to travel that day. Yep, six trains to get me back to Austria. *I had this train time all planned out. This was supposed to be my time to enjoy the journey and reconnect with God. Well, this journey isn't what I had in mind! Twelve hours of travel. Five train connections. Ugh!*

Train number two—Ulm to Augsburg. *God, you have to help me get back to Mödling where at least I know some people and places.*

Train three—Augsburg to Munich. *God, as I board this train, I need to find a seat where I can store all of my luggage above me.* Anytime I entered or exited the train, it felt as if all the people around me stopped to stare. One large backpack on my back and another one strapped to my front.

Train four—Munich to Vienna. *God, would you help me find a seat to myself so I have some space to write in my prayer journal?* It was already after dinner, and the sun had started to set. As I slipped into an empty row of seats, I smiled as I had a few hours to relax and record the day's chaos. Yet I feared the next leg. I didn't have a ticket for that train. I would only have seven minutes to purchase my next ticket and catch the train to Mödling in the Vienna suburbs. *God, I need to get that ticket on the train. I don't have time to go inside the station to purchase a ticket.*

As our train pulled into Vienna Westbahnhof Station, I saw that I had already missed the scheduled departure for the next train to the Vienna Meidling station, taking me to outskirts of the city. *Where would I stay if I couldn't get to Mödling?* I wasn't sure when another train would head that direction. It was as if God planted a question in my mind, *What if that train was late?* The moment the train from Munich came to a halt, I opened the doors, climbed down the train stairs, and ran toward platform two. This required going down stairs, through a small tunnel and up another set of stairs. I was sweating and trying to maintain balance with both of the backpacks I carried. *Who does a workout at eleven p.m.?*

As I climbed the last stair, I noticed the train was still there. Adrenaline kicked in, and I ran toward the first official person I could find.

"Sprechen Sie Englisch?" I asked in a panic.

He looked at me, clearly not excited about this conversation. *Couldn't he tell that I was a single young woman needing to get home?* He must have seen the desperation in my face.

"Where can I buy a ticket for this train? I need to get back to Mödling and have two more trains to get there. Do I have time? Can I get on and then buy a ticket?" He thought for a moment and then waved me on the train. I didn't know that buying a ticket on the train was unheard of; you only pay fines on the train. The worker took the ticket I had in my hand and wrote a message on it in German securing my trip all the way to Mödling.

Train five—Vienna Westbahnhof to Vienna Meidling. *Maybe if I sit as still as possible, no one will ask me for my ticket.* I worried about seeing another worker who wouldn't understand the situation, which I clearly couldn't explain in German. *God, I need You to protect me on this train. Help me get to Mödling.* As we arrived into Meidling, the worker explained *in English* which platform I needed to get to Mödling. I smiled really big and thanked Him again and again.

Train six—Vienna Meidling to Mödling. Finally! My shoulders were so tired from carrying the backpacks from train to train. The one-hour train ride to my final destination seemed to last forever.

The town was quiet. At first, I was so glad to be off of any train it didn't matter much that I couldn't remember how to get back to our house. Then it hit me; I had no idea how to get home. *God, why have I made it this far to only be lost again? All I want is my bottom-bunk IKEA bed. Please, help me find the street back to the house.* My back was sweaty from the backpacks I still carried after six trains and a restless journey. The quiet felt eerie. Blocks away from the train station, I saw a tall man with a dark trench coat and long dark hair. He didn't look like the friendly type. My heart pounded. My pace quickened.

I approached a street sign, *Göethegasse [Ger-tuh-goss-uh]. Yes, that looks familiar! Oh I hope this town follows a grid-system.* I thought about my days living in Chicago and how handy that was when I was lost. As I turned the corner, I saw the yellow A-frame house from a distance. It took everything within me not to squeal with excitement.

By now it was after midnight and everyone was asleep. I wondered if anyone was even worried. I fumbled around the bedroom looking for my headlamp so I could get ready for bed. Courtney and Mallory both stirred in their beds.

"Where have you been?" Courtney asked.

"It's a long story. I'll tell you tomorrow." I responded.

"OK, well I'm glad you're back. Goodnight," she whispered.

As I climbed into the bottom bunk and drifted toward sleep, I smiled. That was definitely not the journey I had hoped for. Yet, somehow in the middle of all my panic and frustration, God guided me and provided what I needed to get home. Even though I had felt distant from Him before, after a weary journey on six trains in two foreign countries, I realized that He was "home" when I wasn't sure I'd ever find my temporary home again. Even when no one else knew where I was, He did.

WHERE IN THE WORLD?

After Christmas, our team headed to Bosnia and Serbia for a two-month outreach focused on children and teens, by hosting fun events and partnering with local churches in order to share God's unconditional love for them. Going into the trip, I knew outreach was a part of the plan, but after finally settling into one culture in Austria, I was about to embark on a trip to visit two new cultures with new languages and customs. Honestly, I wasn't looking forward to it at all. Austria had finally become comfortable after four months, and my homesickness for my American life had waned. Now I would have to start all over and adjust to a new place. Not to mention our entire team was tired of being together *all* the time. Living in close quarters and with little downtime brought out the worst in me.

One night after arriving in our second outreach location, Leskovac, Serbia, I tried to address a conflict I had with Courtney. We had similar personalities, both stubborn and both wanting to take control and create organization out of chaos. As the intensity rose, I realized I wasn't getting anywhere in this conversation, my frustration mounting even with the entire missions training program.

I was supposed to be serving dessert to a group of Serbian churchgoers in their basement-level fellowship hall. But I couldn't be in that church building one second more.

So I ran.

Up the stairs and out the front door of the church.

It was early evening and cold; the sun had gone down about an hour ago. I didn't bother taking my coat. I didn't even know where I was running to and ended up at a playground down the street. As I sat on a swing, I sobbed and shivered. *God, what am I doing here?*

I started to push off of the ground to let the swing take me away from this place, if even for a moment.

Why in the world did You bring me to this program? I'm older than Courtney and Mallory, shouldn't I be an example? I don't even know what to do with the anger and frustration I feel right now. What is wrong with me? I feel as though I've failed You.

I pumped my legs. Stronger and stronger. Higher and higher. Finally, I let my legs hang as the swing began to slow down. I desperately wanted someone to come looking for me. I wanted someone to come up to me and say, "I'm so glad you're here" or "I'm thankful for you." When no one came, I took a deep breath and slowly walked back to the church. *God, You knew where I was, when I was all alone on that train journey. Are You here? Do You see me? This isn't what I thought it would be.*

GOD AND THE DISCO

Instead of embracing the outreach experience, my heart disengaged. I wanted the next step. A ministry organization in England had offered me two positions. I also had the option of joining the leadership of the Mödling missions training program or returning to Vienna with a different missions organization, Greater Europe Mission (GEM), which focused primarily on starting new churches in unchurched areas and mentoring those who call themselves Christ-followers.

Even before we left for Bosnia and Serbia, I Skyped with a woman who had lived in Austria for more than three years and worked for GEM discipling teens. After our conversation, I knew GEM was the next step.

GEM connected me with its team in Vienna; we would meet when I returned to Austria. GEM let me know up front that I'd have to go through an acceptance process and then begin raising financial support. So in Serbia, I found myself distracted by dreams of being back in Austria on a long-term basis by the end of the year.

But God had other plans for the here and now.

I met Susa.

Susa was a sixteen-year-old teen girl living in a mid-size Serbian town. She was all-girl, shy, quiet, and spoke little English, but somehow God gave us a connection. Each time Susa and I met, something about our encounters energized me. I forgot about my frustrations. I forgot about moving onto my "next step." I even forgot about any lingering homesickness, not recognizing if I longed more for Austria or America.

One evening, Susa, her friend Tamara, and I went to a café called The Ship. The décor inside gave the feeling of embarking on a getaway cruise. After ordering my favorite drink in Serbia—dark hot chocolate, which is more like hot, dark chocolate pudding—we walked upstairs to what is known as the "D" deck and sat down to enjoy our drinks. Tamara spoke fantastic English, so she was able to help Susa and I communicate. Ironically, one of our conversations was about Vienna. Susa dreamed of living there someday.

"Susa, what do you like to do for fun?" I asked.

Susa looked at Tamara and started to respond in Serbian. While she couldn't speak much English, Susa often understood basic questions.

"Susa likes to dance on Saturday evenings at the disco in town," Tamara responded.

"OK," I slowly replied. "Tell me about that. How often do you go?"

I slurped more of my dark hot chocolate while Tamara translated, and I tried to see if I could pick out any familiar Serbian words.

"She likes to go every Saturday night with her friends," Tamara said.

Dancing. Hmm. Well, that's a new ministry opportunity I haven't tried out, I thought to myself. I was drawn to this girl. She wasn't one who wanted to be inside the walls of a church, but she loved the disco.

God, I can't believe I'm about to say this. "Susa, could I go with you sometime? I would like to meet your friends."

Susa's eyes lit up. She shook her head yes. I could tell she was excited. Maybe it was something rather special to bring an American to the disco. Or for that matter, three Americans. Courtney and Mallory didn't know it yet, but they were going with me.

That next week, my focus diverted from long-term planning to finding something to wear to the disco. Courtney, Mallory, and I went shopping, and I found some brown boots. Everyone in Europe wore leather boots and skinny jeans before they were even a fashion trend in the U.S. I tried to make do with the jeans I had. Luckily, I had grown up in the '80s and had learned how to tight roll my jeans. (You better believe that's how I got them into my boots!)

I had arranged to meet Susa right outside the church where we were living. The church used to host a Bible school so they had rooms in their basement filled with bunk beds. When Susa arrived, in her best English she tried to introduce us to her friend. Then she motioned for us to start walking down the street toward the disco. While we walked, Susa locked her left arm with my right arm as if we were preparing to square dance. I wasn't sure how to respond at first, but smiled. In Serbia, this means friendship.

The music had already started at the disco, and the teens were piling in. We found a standing table toward the back of the room and ordered some sodas.

I'd need all the caffeine I could get! The music grew louder and louder, and the room became rather crowded and warm.

At one point in the evening, I looked over at Mallory. A guy had approached her and began speaking Serbian. I'm not sure if he understood any English. The next thing I knew, I heard Mallory yelling over the loud music, "I'm here to tell people about Jesus!" As the guy walked away, probably realizing he wouldn't understand what she was saying, everyone at our table broke into laughter.

When a famous Serbian pop singer's music started blaring, Susa's smile grew. This music had a mix of jazz, funk, and Latin-flavor. Courtney, Mallory, and I spent most of the evening dancing with our standing table. We'd watch as Susa would venture out to the dance floor and to other parts of the room to greet friends. This wasn't our thing, but our hope was that by coming she would understand we cared.

The next day, I replayed my evening with Susa.

God, how can You use me in Susa's life? She rarely understands what I'm even saying with the language barrier. What's the next step? I want her to know You. I want her to sense You pursuing her. I want her to experience You. Hmm… how do I experience You? In how You provide. In what You say to me in Your Word. In how You lead me on an adventure. In the purposes You have for my life. I wonder if she knows You have a purpose for her. Help her to know You created her specifically for yourself. I want her to know You like that.

As I prayed, I began to draw stick figures in my journal. One representing Susa and the other representing God. In one scene I drew a brick wall between the two stick figures. *Could I ask her through a simple drawing to tell me what this wall was between her and God?*

A couple of weeks later, I met Susa at another café in town. Even though it was February, the temperature and sunshine made it rather warm that day. I grabbed a table outside the café and waited for Susa to arrive. In my head, I questioned how I had even made a difference in this community with such language barriers. I would only be in Serbia a few more days. Looking over my stick figures one last time, I wondered, *Would she even understand this?* I set my Serbian-English dictionary atop the table. *Maybe we can use this to fill in some of the communication holes.*

I saw Susa quickly coming down the street. I stood up to greet her. She gave me a kiss on each cheek and then we sat down. She was so excited she could barely hold it in. *God why can't I understand Serbian? Please, just for this moment!*

"Susa, what are you excited about?"

She searched in her head for the English words. She grabbed the dictionary and began looking for the words she wanted to say. "I broke up with my boyfriend," she responded.

I had heard her boyfriend wasn't a great influence, but I didn't expect her to be so excited about this break in relationship status. I must have looked shocked and confused.

Susa picked up the dictionary again, quickly flipping through the pages for the next words. "I follow Jesus on Saturday. We had event at church in different town. I become Christian."

My jaw dropped. I pulled out my stick-figure drawing. I crossed out the brick wall. With a huge smile on her face, she shook her head yes. As we got up to leave the café, I grabbed Susa and hugged her.

God did see me. He didn't need my performance. He didn't even need me to speak Serbian. He only needed me to harness myself to Him and join Him for the ride of my life.

CHAPTER 5

Looking to Land

The LORD had said to Abram, "Leave your native country, your relatives,

and your father's family, and go to the land that I will show you" (Genesis 12:1 NLT).

S tepping off the U-Bahn [underground train], I fumbled for the paper
with the address of the church. After taking the escalator up, I began to
search for the large parking lot and shopping center that Jim, the GEM Austria
director, mentioned in his email. Jim and his wife had lived in Vienna for almost
twenty years.

My six months was up, but this wasn't the end of Austria for me. I hoped it
was only the beginning and was nervous about my appointment to finally meet
the GEM team members living in Vienna.

I don't know why I'm so nervous. God, am I stepping in the right direction? When
I got here for the missions training program, I wasn't even sure I had made the right
decision. And this journey has led to so much brokenness—even in my perspective of You.

I've never been so spent or frustrated in my life. It was difficult to be surrounded by the same people every day for almost six months; You know that. This program wore me out, but it also allowed me to see my selfishness, my pride, and my independence when I really need more dependence on You. Thank You that You don't leave me in my ugliness. Thank You for Your grace. As I prepare to take next steps I feel my insecurities rising. Help me, Jesus.

The large parking lot was deserted at nine a.m. No one seemed to be around since the stores in Austria close on Sundays. The church met in a section of a shopping center. When I saw a couple of people heading into a building, I followed them and thought, *Oh, I hope this is the right place.*

As I glanced to my left, a handful of people were playing instruments and practicing what I assumed were worship songs. They faced rows of chairs that were still being set up. An older gentleman approached me. With a warm smile, the gentleman greeted me with a firm handshake, but I didn't understand what he said. I smiled. My eyes darted around the room. I must have looked out of place because a man dressed in a button-down shirt and slacks who had been engaged in a group conversation broke away and moved toward me.

"Hello. I'm Jim. Are you Krishana? Am I saying that correctly?" he asked as he smiled.

"Yes, I am, and your pronunciation is perfect."

"Come this way, and let me introduce you to my wife, Lynette. You can sit with us during service. Do you have lunch plans after church? We would like to invite you if you have the time."

Prior to landing in a seat next to Lynette, Jim already saw the next person he needed to connect with. He let Lynette take over the conversation, and off he went.

That afternoon, Jim explained more about GEM and their focus in Austria. I wasn't sure what youth ministry would look like, but my passion increased as he talked about the possibilities. This only confirmed the steps I had already taken in the application process with GEM. I wanted to be the next person on their Austrian team.

The following morning it was time to head back to America. Part of me was ready, and the other part of me wanted to stay. While on outreach in Bosnia and Serbia, I had dreamed about the day I'd get to fly back to the U.S. Now it was here, and I found the sad feelings hard to understand. *Won't it be easy to go back to the U.S. where everything is in English? Yet, there is something about Austria that has become a part of who I am.*

As the plane raced toward Denver, my mind raced too. Life in the U.S. would be different. I wasn't the *Brio* associate editor anymore. I didn't have a job. I wouldn't be living in the same house. I couldn't even remember which friend had stored my mattress and box springs. I didn't have a car. I sold it to raise money for the six-month training school. But I did have a bike, my feet, and the bus. I was thankful it was March, and Colorado summertime was just around the corner. I had been used to public transportation in Vienna and walking everywhere.

I'm a planner. I like to know what's next and desire to be one step ahead to protect myself. But as my thoughts did loops and back-flips around all of the logistics I'd have to figure out, I started to get really warm. It felt like the tag on my jeans was rubbing up against my skin causing it to itch. I excused myself from my row and headed toward the lavatory.

Scrunching myself into the small restroom, I lifted my shirt and noticed tiny red dots all over my torso and when I pulled up my pant leg from the ankle toward my knee, again, red dots all over my leg. Hives. If I'm really honest, anxiety gets stuck in my mind and it festers. Anxiety then becomes a vice grip around my body until either the circumstance changes or I finally submit it to God. (One time I wondered whether I was allergic to a couple wasp stings and the anxiety over it caused me to pass out. This is funny now, but then it was scary.)

I headed back to my seat and tried to take deep breaths. I had to put away my journal. Writing and trying to working out the logistics caused more harm than good. This was uncharted territory. I didn't know how to get one step ahead of the unknown.

DOROTHY'S RETURN TRIP

The morning after my arrival in Colorado, I wanted nothing more than to stay in my new bedroom all day. I was Dorothy, longing to go back to Oz. I knew there was no place like home, but I didn't know what geographical location constituted home. *God, I'm anxious and nervous and desire nothing more than to stay right where I am. The moment I go downstairs and get acclimated to being back in the U.S., then everything here will really begin—and that scares me. I realize I have choices to make about how I respond to this transition, but can't I just curl up on this bed, cry, and not go anywhere?*

Eventually, coming out of my room was a necessity. I thought returning to the U.S. would be easy, but I was mistaken. Life in Europe had rubbed off on me, and I missed it. In only six months, I had forgotten how to do certain things, such as how to use an American clothes dryer. We didn't have a dryer in Mödling; all of my clothes had to air-dry. There was also the difference in the pace of life.

America was definitely a busy place of go, go, go and produce, produce, produce. I wanted the stores to be closed on Sundays so I had no excuse but to stay home and rest. In Austria, my perspective of God and my relationship with Him had taken me to a deeper place, where my desire for *be*-ing had increased. But someone with a lot of loose ends in her life made other people uncomfortable. Anyone who wanted to hear about my experience in Austria would stay engaged in conversation only for maybe thirty minutes. Most conversations ended with, "What's next?" When I told them I wanted to go back and wasn't sure what that looked like, they wanted to move on to another topic, one that wasn't so messy.

EXPENSIVE TASTE

Three months passed. My next step with GEM was to attend a candidate orientation where I'd find out more about GEM, and they would find out more about me. Then both of us would decide if this was a mutually good fit.

A couple days before orientation, I had emailed a GEM staff member for an estimate of financial support needed to live in Vienna. I had to pick my jaw up off the ground after reading the response. Austria was one of the most expensive countries in Europe. *Of course, I would have expensive taste!* There was no way I could raise funds exceeding my annual income with *Brio* and get back to Austria. It would take years—and I wanted to go back now.

I went into the orientation with walls up around my heart. I was already convinced on day one that this was not where I was supposed to be. God would have to intervene in a significant way if He wanted me to continue with GEM. But I decided to finish the orientation anyway.

Someone once told me that when you get ready to move forward and are unsure of what that looks like, go back to the last thing you know God told you to do. *I don't think she meant going back physically, but hey, it couldn't hurt.*

One of my last significant decisions happened at Focus on the Family. When I was in those shoes, I knew that leaving my job and heading to Austria was what I needed to do. So on the last day of orientation, I arrived early and ventured across the street to Focus on the Family. I decided I'd take my breakfast, coffee, Bible, and journal into their cafeteria like I used to do most early mornings when I still worked there.

God, this is such a special place to me. I almost feel as if this is holy ground. You met me again and again here. Thank You for the idea to come back. Just like when I walked into that Brio *staff meeting and knew what I needed to do next, I will walk out of this place, into that orientation and know that Austria is where I need to be. But all I see are obstacles; You see beyond the obstacles.*

By the end of the day, both GEM and I had decided we were a match.

HOW DO YOU GET TO GOOD-BYE

I wasn't moving to Austria anytime soon. A year after my candidate orientation with GEM, I had only raised fifty percent of the financial support. I had found a part-time job as an administrative assistant for a nonprofit ministry. And my dad had loaned me his car so I wouldn't have to take the bus any longer.

Having a car also allowed me to move in with a family so I could save money on rent. I guess a family that skydives together, stays together. Lauren, my skydiving buddy, had left for college. Lauren's parents, Mark and Joyce, invited me to live with them and their youngest daughter, Katlin. They not only opened their home, but they also welcomed me as if I were family. Joyce became a mentor to me, and many times our early morning coffee conversations would be important reminders of trusting God and not putting so much pressure on myself.

One by one, the families or individuals who participated with me in the GEM orientation raised their support and headed to the field. As each family or person took those next steps, I became discouraged and even questioned God's direction. I found myself crying out to God and sometimes just crying. I couldn't shut down my thoughts about fundraising success and the next step. It consumed me. I was determined. And sometimes that determination caused me to seek success in my own strength.

You really want me in Austria? Are You sure? Because I'm not sure where this money is gonna come from. God, I've met with everyone I know in this town and then some. My performance mentality kicked right back in, *What else do I need to do? I'm running out of options in Colorado. I must not be good enough for God to make this happen. I must have done something wrong. What now? I don't even know what to say or how to pray anymore. Why won't You move this financial mountain and get me back to Austria? Isn't that where You want me? I don't understand!*

As I drove around town early on a Sunday morning, God got my attention. I noticed a couple on a tandem bike. Their legs moved in sync like a dance, yet with such power to propel them mile after mile. I wondered about their story. Were they a married couple who had found this hobby to enjoy together? How did they move together on that bike, making it look so easy? How did the woman on the back know what to do when she couldn't see anything but the guy in front of her? They had to trust each other. God was calling me into that kind of connection with Him, an intimate relationship. He knew I certainly longed for that. *Jesus, what does it look like to move as You move? To go deeper with You?* Little did I know He was going to take everything I had experienced about tandem living thus far, and take it up a notch.

After concluding a long phone conversation with my mom, I knew she was right, but I didn't want to admit it. I needed the help and support of my family in this final push toward Austria. Moving back to Indiana and living with my parents was the best route to continue raising support. Yet, moving forward also meant letting go of what was. Colorado was where I really became an adult: I had my first full-time job, lived with some incredible women, found ways to celebrate the little things in life, learned more about the outdoors than I ever knew, and began my tandem journey with God. *How can I leave, God?* And yet, He was telling me, *Krishana, how can you stay?*

CHAPTER 6

Try, Try Again

Jesus looked at them intently and said, "Humanly speaking,

it is impossible. But with God everything is possible" (Matthew 19:26 NLT).

The Indiana I left when I was eighteen wasn't the same Indiana I returned to at twenty-nine. Most of my friends were married and had children, and many didn't even live nearby. My parents had moved to a different area, so I found it difficult to navigate around town. I often asked my childhood friend, Erin, how to get places I should've known.

I wrote the word *stress* countless times in my prayer journal after arriving in Indiana. Fundraising still consumed me—doing anything to make something happen. I joined a Bible study, thinking it would be an easy way to find women to be a part of my support team. I'd create a deadline to have all my support raised, and the date would pass. I'd create another one; then it too would pass. It was as if I was trying to push a tandem bike up the financial mountain.

My frustration grew and I began to fear that no one would believe that Austria was where God would have me next. Even I struggled to believe it.

God, did I hear You correctly? You created this universe out of thin air. Can't You create financial support out of thin air? Everything I'm doing to raise funds feels like never enough.

I grabbed my Bible and began reading in Isaiah 41: "…So that people may see and know, may consider and understand, that the hand of the LORD has done this, that the Holy One of Israel has created it" (v. 20).

I paused as I reread, "The hand of the LORD has done this."

God, be the Author of this story toward Austria so that others will realize it's Your doing, not mine. I know, this isn't supposed to be about me. You haven't asked me to push the tandem bike up the hill. Help me to stay connected to You. Help me to trust You and the relationship we have.

BACK HOME IN INDIANA

I was trying to fit into a life that felt temporary, yet still held a part that resonated with who I had become. At least I still had the chance to be a part of youth ministry.

Before I left Colorado, I contacted the youth pastor of the church I'd be attending. He wasn't sure about me coming onboard since I had plans for leaving and the timeline was not fixed. However, after we met, he saw my excitement and passion for serving teens and decided to take a risk on me. Here was my chance to break in as a new youth leader, at least for a few more months. I also hoped this would be another opportunity to gather financial support.

I walked up to the door and rang the doorbell. I gripped the Tupperware container full of onions I had chopped, waiting for someone to answer. When I had asked Tammy, the youth leader hosting the youth group party, what I could contribute for taco night, she suggested onions. *Really? Onions!* I thought. *Is this evening going to be worth all the tears I had from these onions?*

Tammy, a blonde in her mid-forties, opened the door.

"Hello. Come on in," she motioned me toward her living room as she hurried back to the kitchen. "Sorry, I have to get the taco shells out of the oven."

"No problem. Where would you like the onions?" I asked showing her my container. I wanted to find out if that was a typical task for new youth leaders, but I didn't know Tammy, so I didn't risk the joke.

"Oh, you can take that downstairs. We'll be hanging out in the basement. My sister, Denise, is down there. Ask her where to put them. Thanks."

As I walked down the stairs, the sounds of sports commentators got louder. The game was on TV. A few teens had arrived and were busy playing Ping-Pong. I headed toward the food and saw Denise, also a blonde who was maybe in her mid-thirties, chatting with a group of youth leaders.

"Hi, Denise. I was told to bring you the onions."

"Hi. OK," she searched the area, "Um, you can put them there," pointing to a spot next to the tomatoes. She went back to the story she was telling and now I wondered what to do.

I walked toward the drinks and scanned the room for someone else I knew. Someone who knew my name. Erin and her husband were the only ones who fit that category, but they were involved in another conversation. I grabbed a Coke and stood behind the couch watching the TV, hoping someone would approach me soon.

More and more teens piled into the basement. There were too many for Ping-Pong now, so I meandered toward a group also standing around like me.

"Anyone want to play a game?" I pointed to the *Apples to Apples* box on a table in the corner. Before long, I was in a circle of teens, sitting on the floor and laughing with them.

Later that evening, I noticed Tammy hovering around the food, putting items away and cleaning up splashes of salsa and sour cream on the counter.

"Could I help you with anything?" I asked.

"It's Krishana, right?"

"Yep, that's right."

"Krishana, if you wouldn't mind gathering empty cups and plates to throw them away, that would be great. Thanks," she responded.

I gathered what I could find and headed back toward Tammy.

"Have you served in youth ministry long?" I asked as I shoved the garbage into the trash can.

"Not exactly," she said. "What about you?"

"I was a youth leader in Colorado before moving here."

"What brought you to Indiana?"

"I'm actually from this area, and my family lives here. I'm preparing to move to Vienna as a missionary but need to complete my fundraising goal before I can leave."

"Wow. I've never been to Austria," she replied. "My family and I went on a missions trip a few years ago to help with a church in Maine. Did I hear you recently traveled to Austria?"

"Yes, right after Christmas. I'd love to tell you more about Austria sometime, if you're interested."

"That'd be great."

The conversation quickly ended as the hometown team scored a touchdown and cheers filled the room.

Before the night ended, Denise approached me.

"I heard you'd like to meet with me and my sister, Tammy, about a missions trip you're taking," she said as she handed back my Tupperware container, still quite full of onions. "Tell me about that."

I smiled inside. Two new friends (even though I wouldn't be staying in town long). *Thank You, Jesus.*

JANUARY TRADITIONS

Turns out I was going to be in town much longer than I expected. In order to stay in Austria for more than three months, I needed a resident permit. The application process for this particular permit started in January every year, and Austria only issued a small number per calendar year. My first attempt was applying at the Austrian Consulate in Los Angeles, California, even before I left Colorado. Unfortunately, my application didn't arrive in Vienna in time to be processed. All of the permits had already been claimed.

Round two: Now, a year later, I lived in Indiana. Jim, the GEM Austria director, researched the permit situation a little more and discovered my best chance to get a resident permit was to stand in line on January 2 outside of the government office in the heart of Vienna. We decided I could combine this trip with attending their team retreat.

I gathered my paperwork and took it with me to Vienna for ten days.

That's where Jim, Dawn, and I stood outside in the bitter cold for an hour or so before they unlocked the building to let us in. Dawn, my oncology nurse friend, a brunette with shoulder-length hair, dressed in a white puffy coat, didn't talk much. She sipped her coffee.

I hesitated to say anything to her, but it seemed awkward to listen to the men in our group chatter away while we stood in silence. I decided to take the risk.

"So how many layers did you put on?" I asked.

"Too many to count," she responded. "But I forgot to bring the foot warmers for inside of my shoes. My feet are freezing!"

Dawn went back to sipping her coffee in between our brief conversation while waiting for the doors to open.

When the doors opened, we went from freezing to sweating in a matter of minutes. The heaviest layers came off as we stood in line to receive a number. This number would show up on a screen to let us know we could approach that office and turn in our paperwork.

As I approached the front of the line, Jim interrupted my thoughts. "Krishana, the piece of paper they will give you is extremely important. The number is your place in line. If you lose this piece of paper you are no longer in line."

The man behind the counter handed me a small piece of paper. I looked down to see what it said: 007.

This had to be a good sign. Right, God? Surely this wouldn't be an impossible mission any longer with a 007 like me!

I couldn't stop smiling.

Our group took the elevator upstairs. As we entered the waiting room, you could have heard a pin drop. The only sounds were papers shuffling. I looked around the room to see many ethnicities and families, all applicants, probably as nervous as I was and wondering if they had all of the documentation the Austrian government would ask for. Every so many minutes, a new number would appear on the screen telling that person to head to Office 100 or Office 102.

"Krishana, do you still have your number?" Jim asked. This was at least the third time he had asked since we had been downstairs.

"Yes, I have it right here in my pocket," I responded, barely pulling it out to show him. "Good, you will have to turn it in when we get to our assigned office," he said. "I wouldn't want you to lose your place and have to wait another year to apply."

I smiled nervously.

Finally, our turn arrived. I let Jim do all the talking. I smiled at the woman behind the desk and pulled out each document Jim needed as we made the transaction. I'm not sure if that was the hard part or if waiting two to three months was more difficult.

As we headed back outside to leave, Jim gathered our group in front of the building, which displayed leftover Christmas decorations, to document the moment with a photo.

"Really, Jim. It's freezing!" Dawn complained. "This isn't the best time for a picture."

I could tell the caffeine had kicked in and Dawn was more awake, but she didn't want to stand in the cold after finally getting warm inside.

"You will want this for your supporters," Jim responded as he showed us where to stand.

Unfortunately, neither that picture perfect moment nor my stealthy 007 aided this mission. The paperwork was processed this time, but about a month later I found out they wanted more documentation. Back for another year in Indiana.

THE WORST TIME OF THE YEAR—ROUND THREE

A year later, Jim mentioned that January would arrive soon. Once again I'd need to be in front of that government building early in the morning on the day it opened after the holidays. This time we decided we would maximize the cost of a plane ticket; he would help arrange for me to stay in Vienna for five weeks, long enough to complete my first month of language school and again attend the GEM-Austria team retreat.

On New Year's Day, I was in Vienna again. January weather is bitter cold and windy with mostly gray skies. I think the GEM-Austria team was surprised I continued to come back every dreary January.

Jim helped me load my luggage into the car, and we headed toward the twenty-first district of Vienna. It wasn't until then that Jim told me about the Austrian woman I would be staying with for the month.

"Waltraude is in her late sixties. She has attended our church for many years and is quite involved. She does speak English but will speak mostly German so you can be immersed in the language," Jim informed me. "By the way, the last young woman who stayed with her left a candle burning and set a little fire in her room. I wouldn't advise burning any candles."

I nodded my head and tried to take all of this information in as my palms started to get sweaty. *Oh dear Jesus, I'm starting from scratch with German. How will we even communicate? She hasn't even met me, but because of her last experience she may not be happy about this arrangement.*

Jim wedged himself and my large suitcase in the tiny elevator at Waltraude's apartment complex. As the elevator doors closed, he said, "Come to the fourth floor." I waited as the elevator went up and then came back down. I stepped into the small elevator and pulled my carry-on items in with me. *What if she doesn't like me? What would this experience say about my qualifications as a missionary?* My heart beat faster as I passed each floor.

Once I reached the fourth floor, Jim pressed a button outside of the door. A woman with short gray hair greeted us with a smile and motioned for us to come in. Jim and Waltraude immediately spoke German at a pace faster than I could even try to comprehend.

As we brought my luggage into the guest room, I immediately saw a candle burning. I gasped inside. *Is she setting me up for failure?*

Jim and Waltraude discussed where I would need to be in two days, back in front of that government building bright and early. Then Jim said his good-byes and headed home. Waltraude pointed to things in the cheery, yellow room and identified them in German so I would understand. She showed me where I could put my clothes and unpack my belongings. Next to a twin bed, she had a desk in front of a window looking out to another apartment building. We then headed to the kitchen.

"Trinkst du Kaffee?" Waltraude asked pointing to the coffee maker.

"Ja," I responded. *Yes, I like to drink coffee but not now.*

I watched intently looking for clues as to whether she meant right now or in the morning. She showed me the ground coffee, the filters, and where to put the water. *OK, so she's not making coffee. She must mean in the morning.*

After a tour of her apartment, I motioned that I would start unpacking and get ready for bed.

"Gute Nacht," she chimed.

"Gute Nacht," I replied.

The moment she was gone, I blew out the candle. Talk about not wanting your first real experience living with an Austrian to go up in flames.

Two days later, I got up around four a.m. and had to leave rather early to stand in line once again for my resident permit. I quietly tiptoed around the place, making sure I had every document ready for inspection. I put on many layers of clothing, found my boots by the front door, and headed out into the hallway. The hallway was black. I couldn't even see my hands in front of my face. I remember seeing Jim press a button in the hallway that turned on the hall lights. The light switches looked different from the ones I was accustomed to. I think the button he pressed in the hallway was a small circular one.

I scanned the wall to find one of these magic buttons. I noticed a red button lit up. *That couldn't be it. That button looked dangerous.* I ran my hands along the wall and found a circular button. *This must be it.* The moment I pressed it, I realized there was no turning back. Instead of light, I heard a loud buzz coming from inside the door I had just closed. Waltraude's doorbell!

Oh no! I paused to see if she would come to the door. No one stirred. I locked the front door and instead of trying to find another button, blindly found my way to the elevator. As I got in the elevator and tried to calm my heart after the doorbell adrenaline rush, I thought, *I'm not off to a good start. I have to find a way to apologize before language school. Do I go back in and write her a note?*

The voice that spoke the loudest was Jim's, making sure I wasn't late to stand in line. I hurried along, knowing I'd have plenty of time to think about this situation while waiting for the doors of the Austrian government building to open. This time, though, I was the only candidate Jim had to talk to at six a.m.

"Jim, did you drink coffee before you left the house?" I asked.

"I rarely drink coffee. I'm what you would call a social coffee drinker," he replied with a chuckle.

With an emphasis on social, I thought as I grinned.

As the doors opened, my heart wasn't pounding like the last time. We approached the desk to acquire a number. Once my number appeared on the screen, Jim and I headed toward Office 102. As he knocked and opened the door, as is customary in Austria before entering a place of business, the meeting began.

"Grüß Gott [*Groose Got*]," Jim greeted those in the office.

"Grüß Gott [Good day]," the woman behind the desk replied.

I shuffled in behind him. It was hard to imagine I'd ever be confident in a situation like this. I felt as if one wrong move, and I would be deported. Jim carried the conversation and motioned to me when I needed to hand in the documents.

After our short exchange of information, he and I both shook hands with the woman behind the desk.

"Dankeschön. Wiedersehen *[Dahn-kuh shurn. Vee-dair-zayn]*," Jim remarked as he headed toward the door.

"Dankeschön. Wiedersehen [Thank you. Good-bye]," I quickly chimed in as I followed him back to the waiting room.

"Wiedersehen," I heard the woman behind the desk reply as we closed the office door.

Now all we could do was wait—about two or three months.

I rushed back to Waltraude's apartment, which meant taking two U-bahns

and a Straßenbahn (streetcar). I didn't have much time before class, but I had
already formulated in my head a simple note in English:

*Dear Waltraude, I am sorry for ringing your doorbell this morning before I
left. I hope I did not wake you. I will be home after my language class.*

　　　　　　　　　　　　　　　　　　　　　　—*Krishana*

With no one home, I left the note on the kitchen counter and headed to
the Vienna city center for language school. Someone had told me that as you
walk down the city streets in Vienna, you should always look up because the
architecture of the buildings is so detailed and beautiful. I guess I had walked a
little too long looking up, because I failed to notice an important feature about
the building where I would have classes. I had no idea how to open the door.

I pushed the door. I pulled the door. It wouldn't budge. *How in the world do
they expect me to go to language class if I can't get in the building?*

I stepped away from the door and watched as, one by one, students would
approach the door, press a button, a buzzing sound would follow, and then they'd
enter. *Why is it always about pressing some button to get anything to turn on or open?*
I slipped in the door behind one of the students, adding it to my mental list to
ask someone from my class how that worked.

By the time I finished language class, it was dark. I made my way back to
Waltraude's on public transportation. I wished I could fall asleep on the bus and
someone would wake me up at the Kagraner Platz stop. But I was afraid I would
miss it, so I kept myself wide-eyed, praying along the way that I would be able to
find Waltraude's apartment once again.

I walked in the door and saw my note still on the kitchen counter.

Oh no! Either she didn't read it, didn't understand it or she wants to talk about it.

After taking off my coat, hat, scarf, and especially my shoes, which is typical in most Austrian homes, I grabbed the note and walked into the living room to find Waltraude lounging on the sofa.

"Waltraude."

"Krishana! Wie geht es dir? Hast du in der Sprachschule viel gelernt? [How are you? Did you learn a lot in language school?]"

I had no idea what she is saying.

"Um," I pointed to my note. "Did you see my note? I rang the doorbell this morning and thought the sound would wake you."

"Nein. Ich höre fast gar nichts wenn ich schlafe. [I hear almost nothing when I'm sleeping.]" she replied.

OK, so she said no. And she's smiling. Everything must be OK.

I smiled.

"Möchtest du Fernseh schauen? [Do you want to watch TV?]" Waltraude asked pointing to the TV.

"OK," I replied. My brain was so tired after a three-hour class. At least I could mindlessly watch the TV, and not worry about my struggle to understand or speak German in conversation.

As I watched, Waltraude would laugh, and then I would smile. I barely understood the humor, but it delighted my heart to watch her eyes and face light up when something funny happened. *God, this living arrangement with Waltraude scared me to death. Live with an Austrian woman for five weeks? I thought Jim had to be out of his mind. But now I sit here and marvel at the ways she makes me feel at home here, inviting me to join her. Thank You.*

German swirled in my head as I collapsed in bed, and as tired as I was, I couldn't seem to turn off my mind. I was thankful for the upcoming holiday, so I could take a breath before starting a new week in this new place.

A DAY IN THE LIFE

I learned quickly that collapsing into bed was a natural part of my weekday routine. Each morning began with my attempt to make coffee.

"Krishana, der Kaffee ist nicht stark genug. [The coffee isn't strong enough.]" she said after the first attempt.

Then the next day I adjusted the coffee-to-water ratio and the pendulum swung the other direction. "Krishana, wir trinken Kaffee, der so stark ist, nur am Nachmittag. [Krishana, we only drink coffee that strong in the afternoon.]" she said after taking a sip.

The third attempt, I instead paused in front of the coffee maker. "Möchtest du mich Kaffee machen? [Would you like me to make coffee?]" I asked in broken German.

Waltraude's eyes looked upward as if she reviewed my last two attempts in her mind. She approached the coffee maker where I stood. I watched as she clarified the exact measurement for breakfast coffee and showed me the amount of water to use for both of us to enjoy two cups. This was helpful, but sometimes I would linger in my room longer just so she would take over the coffee prep and I didn't have to start my day worrying about the coffee-to-water ratio.

My day started around seven or eight a.m. If I hadn't completed my language school homework, that was also on the list after breakfast and getting ready for the day. It seemed the only time I wasn't immersed in German was when I was sleeping, and still, basic words and phrases would occasionally show up there as well.

"Guten morgen, Krishana. Hast du gut geschlafen? [Good morning, Krishana. Did you sleep well?]" Waltraude greeted me each morning.

By the second week, I had picked up enough to respond to this question.

"Guten morgen. Ja, ich habe gut geschlafen. [Yes, I slept good.]" I replied.

Once the greetings were exchanged and coffee was available, Waltraude sometimes offered me a soft-boiled egg for breakfast. This included at least forty-five minutes of eating and brief conversation with her at the table. In language school I was learning about the words you use to describe the weather, so that was one topic I could offer for our dining enjoyment. *I wonder if she gets tired of me commenting how gray and cloudy it is outside. It is January!*

One question I was quick to use was "Wie heißt das auf Deutsch? [How do you say that in German?]" This was a great conversation filler when I didn't know what to say. I'd point to something and use this question. This bought me at least five more minutes.

Each week in class, there was a new section and approximately fifty vocabulary words to learn and memorize. *God, help me to learn these. I hate being on the spot in class and not knowing what to say or how to respond. I want to be as prepared as I can for whatever conversation we might have today.*

Around noon, I headed toward the Vienna city center. Most days, I took my packed lunch to the same spot, Michaelerplatz, a circular plaza with a cobblestone street. The backdrop of the plaza had towering columns and ornate arches that marked the entrance to the Hofburg, what used to be the palace/residence of the

Habsburg family who reigned and ruled for centuries. This left me with one hour to eat and people watch before I submerged myself in German listening and speaking for three hours.

By the time class was over, the January sun was long gone, and I would begin the hour journey home—that is if I correctly timed it using public transportation. A stop at the neighborhood Hofer (grocery store) to pick up a few items usually ended most days. My brain hurt by then, but I knew had to make the stop. *God, help me!* was a typical prayer as I walked into a store. I always hoped their computer screen pointed toward me so I could see exactly what my items cost when I didn't understand their German. Cashiers didn't like me so much when I took too much time to hand them my cash. Speediness in the grocery store was a high cultural value.

"Guten morgen, Krishana. Hast du gut geschlafen?" Waltraude asked. It had been almost four weeks since we began this routine.

"Nein." I struggled to think about how to describe the sleep I had last night. "Ich habe nicht so gut geschlafen." I didn't know how to say that I had woken up sweating in the middle of the night. "Krank [Sick]?" I wasn't sure how to form the sentence. It had been freezing outside, so how could I have been sweating? Cracking the window seemed to help a little bit.

PUSHED TO THE EDGE

My five weeks were coming to a close, and my body was worn out. I had pushed myself through language school and adjusted to a culture unlike my own. Tasks such as buying my own food, meeting friends for coffee, and navigating the city of Vienna took more energy than I could have imagined. I felt as though I was coming down with a cold or maybe even strep throat.

As I got ready for bed, I stood in front of the bathroom mirror. *Did I never notice this before? What are these bumps on both sides of neck?*

I walked into the living room and showed Waltraude. I said I had been feeling fatigued and had a bit of a sore throat. As she looked at my lymph nodes, she immediately had a solution to my problem. Knowing I wouldn't understand her prescription, she showed me what to do, pointing to the shower first. Pointing to my towel next, then my pjs and then to a light blanket she had retrieved from a linen closet that she then wrapped tightly around my body.

"Du musst im diese Bettdecke schlafen," she said firmly. I wasn't about to argue. She must know what she's talking about. I honestly didn't have the energy to do anything but obey what she told me to do. Even when it was difficult to communicate, I had grown fond of Waltraude. It was as if she knew what I needed. She didn't coddle me but could tell when I needed a break. This was one of those moments. I saw a soft side to her as she sent me to bed with a "Gute Nacht."

Only a few more days in Vienna, so I had to push through. There wasn't time to pause—God's agenda was on the line. I knew He would be asking me to jump soon.

Just before I left Austria, I found out I had enough financial support to attend missionary training school in North Carolina. The pieces were finally coming together. Soon I would live in Vienna and continue this tandem journey with God. But, first, I needed to feel better. Tomorrow, I'd make a doctor's appointment for the one full day I would be in Indiana. I didn't need anything else slowing me down.

CHAPTER 7

On My Knees

You love him even though you have never seen him. Though you do not see him now,

you trust him; and you rejoice with a glorious, inexpressible joy (1 Peter 1:8 NLT).

B iopsy. I couldn't get the word out of my head. I wished I could hop on one foot, and lean my head over like you do when you have water in your ear and shake it out, but the word remained. I felt even more protective of my body as we drove home to southern Indiana, especially knowing my spleen was larger than before. I hugged a pillow all the way home, using it as a barrier between me and the seatbelt, just in case we had any sudden stops.

I don't remember what we talked about or listened to on the radio, but as much as my sick body allowed, my mind spun with what all of this would mean for moving to Austria. I knew the doctors' appointments would begin again Monday. All I could do until then was rest and join other college basketball fans in watching as much of the NCAA basketball tournament as possible.

On Monday, the doctor ordered a CT scan. Instead of just sitting in the waiting room to drink the oral contrast that they require for the scan, I took it along and went with my mom to her school. She was a teacher and had to take care of a few things to prepare her classroom for the time off she would need to take care of me. I sat in the teacher's lounge and slowly sipped the oral contrast. It did not taste like the Frappuccino drink they had promised it to be. *Jesus, how will I finish this drink without throwing up?* Teachers would come in and out of the lounge, wanting to make conversation. I tried my best to smile. After a minute of looking at me, they knew not to ask any more questions. I wondered if they could see the sickness.

With the CT scan complete, the doctor recommended a lymph-node biopsy. My aunt Kelly coordinated an appointment with one of the best surgeons in Louisville, Kentucky, for the next day. The surgeon examined me and explained the process of how he would remove a lymph node from under my left arm, hinting that this could be lymphoma. That wasn't the first time I had heard this word, but it was the first time I thought, *I could have cancer.* My mom teared up in the exam room. I didn't have energy for tears. I just wanted to feel better. Tomorrow: surgery. No time to chew and swallow the *lymphoma* word.

Within seventy-two hours I had been required to fast twice for medical procedures. Hungry and tired, I watched as the clock ticked by, wondering when the next procedure would be over, and that's when I was greeted by a familiar face. Sarah would be my nurse through this process, and we had gone to high school together. Something was so comforting about seeing her. I put aside my game-face and relaxed. *God, thank You for bringing Sarah today. You knew I needed a familiar face.*

The biopsy confirmed the surgeon's suspicions. This was a type of non-Hodgkin's lymphoma. My family waited by my side as I awoke from anesthesia to tell me the news and the next step—an oncology appointment the following week.

A CROSSROADS

The uncomfortable tension at home began after that biopsy. Neither my parents nor I knew what to talk about or what to say. We tried to let the sounds of the NCAA tournament drown out our heads and our hearts. However, we couldn't escape cancer. It found us no matter how hard we tried. I've never seen so many cancer commercials on TV as I did between the time I had the biopsy and when I would meet with the oncologist.

On the verge of an official diagnosis, my game-face remained. I wondered if everyone was thinking, *When is she finally going to break down?* Give way to anything but my stoic expression meant cancer was a reality. A reality I didn't know how to handle.

One morning, I slipped into the bathroom to be alone. I wanted to process the last week. I wanted to talk to God about this medical whirlwind. I stood in front of my bathroom mirror, like I had in Vienna when Waltraude took care of me. *How can I have cancer? I'm a runner. I lived in Colorado for six years and was active and healthy and allowed all of those who were all about organic rub off on me.* As I looked at myself, I teared up. Many people in our community would be watching me and even from afar through my Tandem Living blog. *How can I do this?*

There wasn't a food or a medicine or a magic solution that I could concoct overnight to fix this. I felt so helpless, so far beyond being in control. The only One I knew who really had any pull in this situation was the One who is always in control. I just thought He always needed my help.

The heaviness of cancer weighed on my shoulders. This diagnosis could take my life. I knelt down on the bathroom rug. I cried, and I prayed. My heart screamed from my bathroom floor. This was a crossroads. Either I would surrender the game-face and let God pull me in close or keep telling myself to stay strong. Would I really push through *cancer*? Or would I embrace tandem living? He wasn't even asking me to pull the 'chute or to even understand this new reality. Even when I couldn't see what was ahead, He wanted me to trust Him. This was an absolute surrender.

HERE'S MY HAND

Two days before my oncology appointment, Tammy called.

"Krishana, I'm so sorry you're dealing with cancer," she began.

I wasn't sure what to say.

She quickly filled the silence, "When is your appointment with the oncologist?"

"March 16," I responded.

"Do you know what questions to ask?"

"I'm not sure where to even begin."

While I had only heard snippets before this conversation, Tammy began to share her story and experience with cancer. She was a mom of a seven-year-old cancer survivor. Her youngest son, Joshua, had been diagnosed with cancer at ten months old. She had so many tips and suggestions. As she talked, I could tell she knew what she was talking about. Here I was this international traveler, yet she was well traveled in cancer: she knew what to pack, what to ask, and even the kinds of foods that would be good. Our phone conversation lasted two hours. I'm not sure we had ever talked that long.

The next evening, Tammy and her high school daughter Danielle, showed up at our front door. Tammy wanted to get the final "packing-list items" into my hands. We sat on the couch, and she handed me a large white binder. She had slipped a yellow paper inside the front plastic cover that said, "Krishana, 'So do not fear, for I am with you; do not be dismayed, for I am your God. I will strengthen you and help you; I will uphold you with my righteous right hand' (Isaiah 41:10). Love, Jesus." Tammy didn't know that when I had laid awake at night in North Carolina, wondering what my body was going through, God had already been speaking this over me: *I will hold your hand, Krishana.*

The binder had a spot for almost every type of document I would acquire during a cancer journey. It had a section labeled *Doctor's Visits* where I could write questions and record information; a section to keep track of the medications I was taking; a section to keep my results from scans, blood tests, etc., and even a section to organize the medical bills I would receive months later. I saw another yellow paper stuck inside the front pocket on which Danielle had typed out encouraging verses and quotes.

STEROID MASH

As my parents and I walked down the hall toward the oncology office, I was nervous. When we opened the door, a friendly receptionist, Connie, greeted us. While I checked in, she made conversation with my parents and offered us something to drink. No one else was in the office at the time. It was just us, and I was thankful.

"Ms. Kraft," the nurse technician called.

She brought me into a small room and pointed toward the scale. I stepped up, nervous to see how much more weight I had lost. My clothes felt loose. At first I thought this was the result of a month of walking around Vienna, but even after returning to the States, I noticed my weight dropping a half-pound to a pound per day.

After taking my blood pressure and temperature, she led me and my parents to a small exam room.

"Don't worry about undressing now, Dr. J would like to meet with you first," she said as she pulled the door shut.

Moments later, a tall woman with curly blonde hair came in, dressed in a white coat, worn over a long dress, pantyhose, and heels. My mom had her pen and paper handy, including a tape-recorder, just as Tammy had suggested so we wouldn't miss anything the doctor had to say.

After her initial greetings, she explained this type of non-Hodgkin's lymphoma in as simple terms as she could. My type of cancer was Follicular lymphoma, which more typically showed up in people over age sixty. It's usually a slow-moving cancer, but after another scan, she would know more. I liked the way she explained what was happening in my body. It didn't feel like a foreign language.

What came out of her mouth next surprised me, "What are your plans or dreams for the future?"

I sat there dumbfounded. *My plans? Aren't my plans irrelevant now?* I thought. "Well, I had hoped to move to Vienna, Austria, in May as a missionary," I responded.

"We might need to put that off for six months," she said. Her voice was full of hope and gentleness. She wanted to help me toward health so I could do exactly what my heart desired. *God, this conversation is blowing my mind! Are You serious? Austria isn't out of the picture?*

Our final moments with Dr. J mapped out the days to come, including another "dreaded opportunity" to fast and have a PET scan. (I didn't enjoy giving up meals.) Before I left, Dr. J said I needed a pneumonia vaccine before chemotherapy treatments destroyed my immune system. She took me to a little treatment room where I met Nurse Kim for the first time. Petite like me, this brunette entered the room with an upbeat expression and attitude. In my head, I remembered something Tammy had mentioned, *Your oncology nurses are some of your most valuable sources of information. Don't hesitate to ask them questions.* She was confident in what she was doing and yet very gracious knowing we were overwhelmed, confused, and fearful.

God, I hope when I come back for treatment that Kim will be here.

Less than twenty-four hours following my PET scan, Dr. J called my cell phone.

"Krishana, after reviewing your PET scan results, I want to start treatment immediately. As in next week. Between your blood tests and the PET scan, we've detected lymphoma cells in your bone marrow. This is quite serious but very treatable. I would like to schedule an outpatient surgery to put in a port on Monday and begin treatment on Tuesday. Can we begin this process?"

I stood by the kitchen table holding onto the closest chair. I swallowed hard. *God, this is worse than Dr. J imagined? Help me.*

"Yes, you can make those appointments for me," I replied.

"OK, Connie will call you back with the details. We will see you in our office next week," Dr. J said.

And with that my life as I knew it changed. I posted an update on my Tandem Living blog. Soon after, I received an email from Dawn, my future teammate living in Austria. With her oncology expertise, she wrote:

One thing you could ask the surgeon—after he places the port, he will have to check for correct placement. Ask him to Hep-Lock it and leave the port accessed for your chemo tomorrow. Sometimes they don't know when chemo is scheduled to start, and it's better if he can leave the Huber needle in the port overnight so it will be better for you tomorrow. Don't worry if he can't/doesn't want to, it's just helpful for you and the nurses tomorrow.

—Love, Dawn

Hep-Lock, accessed, Huber needle? She might as well have written in German. I printed the email and took it with me to the hospital. Hopefully, someone would understand what this meant. All I knew is that it could make my first treatment easier, and since I didn't even understand what chemo really meant, easier sounded good.

The night before my port surgery, my brother and his family came to visit me. I wouldn't be able to spend time with my nephew Kaleb following treatment because my immune system would be compromised, and I would be susceptible to germs. I had been told that Kaleb prayed for me, with as many words and understanding that a four-year-old could handle. He didn't understand what was going on or even what cancer meant. But he knew that his Aunt Kishy was sick.

"Kaleb, do you remember the song about how God is bigger than the boogie-man?" I asked.

"Yes," he looked at me with wide eyes.

"Well, our God is also bigger than the cancer boogie-man," I told him.

I could see he was thinking about what I had said. He smiled, motioned for a high-five and said, "Niiiice!"

I hugged him tightly. To think my big God would use this little guy to pray for me. *I'm overwhelmed by You.*

Within a week, I had a lymph node taken out from under my left arm and a port placed below my collarbone on my left side. My body was tired, but I had to keep going. I needed treatment to kill the cancer cells taking over my body.

My first chemo treatment began at nine a.m. the next day. The car ride from southern Indiana to the east end of Louisville was a long and nauseating journey. I had tried to gulp down the steroid pills that morning after eating, but I did not feel good sitting in the back seat of my parents vehicle. I asked my dad to stop and get me a Sprite at a gas station on the way. I sipped the soda and prayed that I would hold down the medication. Every movement from the car made me want to throw up.

I tried to smile when I arrived at the oncology office, especially when I saw Nurse Kim walk into my treatment room. She explained the process and told me to pay attention to my body and how it was responding—and to report anything and everything. She brought a calmness with her.

The treatment took seven hours. Some of the cancer drugs made me throw up immediately. Other moments, I felt shortness of breath or symptoms of an allergic reaction. For seven hours!

I was thankful when I climbed into my bed that night. Although I had to go back to the oncology office the next day to get fluids, at least I wasn't going back for chemo for three more weeks—no appointment, surgery, scan, or treatment until then. I pulled my Bible into bed with me. It fell open to Nehemiah 8. As I skimmed the page, verse 10 was underlined, "The joy of the LORD is your strength." I smiled. *Yes, Jesus. I'm not sure what that even looks like today.*

This was a free fall. You can't prepare for a free fall. All you can do is hang on.

CHAPTER 8

Peace in the Pieces

Don't worry about anything; instead, pray about everything.
Tell God what you need, and thank him for all he has done.
Then you will experience God's peace, which exceeds anything we can
understand. His peace will guard your hearts and minds as you
live in Christ Jesus (Philippians 4:6–7 NLT).

I sat on the floor surrounded by a group of teen girls and a handful of female youth leaders who were all spending the weekend together in a cabin in Nashville, Indiana, for our annual high school girls' retreat.

Before I began to share about my cancer journey, I handed a puzzle piece to each person in the room.

"If this puzzle piece represents one piece to the huge puzzle-story of your life, for you, what does your piece represent? What is that circumstance or fear you face right now?"

I could feel the silence in the room as each girl held her piece of the puzzle.

"I once held a puzzle piece I'd call cancer and fear of the unknown," I said to break the silence. "Hold your puzzle piece in your hand. What's the hard part about only having one piece to the puzzle?"

"Um, you're not quite sure what the entire puzzle will be?" one teen girl offered as a guess.

"Yes," I responded. "Becoming a young woman of peace means filling in the unknowns with God. If *that* happens. Fill in the "that" with any type of difficult circumstance. I know I still have God. Deuteronomy 31:6 says, 'Be strong and courageous. Do not be afraid or terrified because of them, for the LORD your God goes with you; he will never leave you nor forsake you.'

"We have to remember that many times we only hold one piece to the puzzle. We don't know how God is going to use this part of our story for His glory and purpose. We may not always *feel* peaceful, but having God's peace is a bit different. It's a state of calmness because God's Holy Spirit is changing us and helping us to view whatever is happening in light of who He is."

CYCLES OF CHEMO AND FAITHFULNESS

A year ago, my conversations with God looked drastically different. I was trying to figure out support raising and getting to Austria, asking God over and over for guidance in the next step to take. While Austria was still on my mind and heart, it wasn't even on the table now that cancer had taken over.

God, I made it through one chemo. Now I know what chemo is actually like. I feel awful. I don't want to move a muscle. It feels like the moment I do, I'll throw up. Help me know You are near.

Before I knew it, three weeks were up and I laid awake that night before the next round of chemo.

God, how is it that yesterday I enjoyed being outside in the sunshine, walking and talking with Tammy and now I have to start all over? I don't want to feel awful again. I like having my energy back. My heart dreads this next round. This time I know how badly I'll feel afterward. I need You. I need Your help in walking through the yuck.

The next morning, I got up extra early to gather my things and give myself enough time to take the steroid pills required for the first five days in the chemo cycle. The pill bottle taunted me from the counter, "You have to take me, but you know you can't do it without gagging!"

I grabbed the bottle, pulling out one pill and holding it in my hand. How could this tiny pill be such a big obstacle? I placed it in a pill cutter and smashed it, and then scraped every last grain into the small applesauce cup I had ready. I sat at the kitchen table with spoon in hand. Placing the spoon in the applesauce, I scooped a bite. *God, help me to get this down. It's so difficult to give myself something that causes my body to feel out of control.* By the end of the day, I'd have a restless energy that puts caffeine to shame. *God, help me to rest, even on steroids. Will you help me go to sleep—even for an hour? Be my Rest, Lord Jesus.*

Chemo and steroids messed with almost every blood level in my body (white blood count, hemoglobin, iron, potassium, neutrophils, platelets, etc.) Every three weeks, Nurse Kim would check my blood before starting the chemo process. After a couple of rounds, she saw what adjustments I needed to keep me strong.

"Krishana, your iron level is low. We'll need to get you started on an iron supplement," she said.

"Iron? I hear that can really mess with your stomach," I responded.

"Potentially," she said, "But if we don't get your levels up by the next chemo round, we'll have to delay it, which only delays you getting better."

"I understand," I responded with a fake smile. *Another pill, really?!*

One week on a typical iron supplement and my digestive system was in knots.

My childhood friend Erin understood. She was expecting her first child and facing quite a few physical changes herself. We would take walks around her neighborhood and discuss all of our bodily woes, such as constipation. Here we were, two women in our early thirties, discussing bodily functions like we were two old ladies walking around a nursing home. There had to be a better solution to this iron supplement situation. *Show me, God. I'm watching.*

One night as I sat in front of the TV, my ears perked up as I heard the words *iron supplement.*

"Here is a dual iron solution for your sensitive system…" the woman on the TV exclaimed. I grabbed a napkin and wrote down the name of the product.

"Have you ever seen the commercial for this?" I asked Nurse Kim, handing her the info I had printed from my online discoveries.

"No, I haven't. Where did you hear about it?" she asked.

"On TV, while my dad and I watched Jeopardy," I giggled.

"Hmm, this looks legit to me. Let me ask Dr. J what she thinks. If she approves, you're more than welcome to try it," Kim responded with a smile.

I never saw that commercial again. Yet, by my next chemo cycle, with the help of the supplement, my iron had increased and without suffering side effects.

You knew, God, didn't You? I never imagined I'd pray about iron supplements. Yet, now we talk about my body all the time. My time with You used to be primarily about a disciplined routine, but now things are different. I can't go very long without bringing You into something my body is dealing with.

God became my lifeline to whatever practical need my body had in the moment. It reminded me of the day when I traveled on six trains from Germany to Austria, talking to God all the way just to make it home. He knew exactly where I was when no one else did and the details of each day, even the details of my body. He wanted to *be* the focus of my life, not just talk about it.

HE HAS THEM NUMBERED

I sat in the swivel chair in Rachael's garage. This wouldn't be easy. *God, help me to be brave.*

Rachael, and her husband, Cody, had lived in southern Indiana for a couple of years. Cody was the youth pastor at my church; Rachael was my hair stylist. On most appointments she would ask me what I was thinking for my latest style. I'd show her a photo, and we'd go from there.

Today, as usual, she covered me with a black cape. *I can't wait to say something; I have to break the mood of this moment.*

"So, I'm thinking, let's start with a cut that looks like a three-year-old got a hold of some scissors," I piped up. "I want some good photos! Then we can shave it all off from there."

I breathed deeply. *OK, there, no turning back now.* I could see Rachael smile in the mirror.

"OK, let's do it," she responded.

"Recently, I made a video for my blog and so many people had commented how cute my hair was. They thought I had it cut," I filled her in. "I didn't have the heart to tell them my hair was falling out, the longest layers first."

My hair had been falling out for a couple of weeks, and I could no longer handle the hair falling out on my pillow, in my food, everywhere. I had to shave my head.

As Rachael began to take the razor to my head, I swallowed hard. This moment was more difficult than I let my face show. After finishing the last section, she brushed off the back of my neck. There was no need for comments like, "So, what do you think?" or "Is this what you had in mind?"

"Thank you," I said as I put on the bandana I had brought with me. I could see tears pooling in her eyes.

"Of course," she responded. Then I hugged her good-bye.

My vulnerability felt magnified without my hair. I imagined people doing double takes at stoplights as I drove home. I imagined them thinking, *What happened to her hair?*

Losing my hair was the side effect that solidified the cancer diagnosis for me. Other times in my life I had felt sick, had thrown up, had a sore throat, etc. but I had never lost my hair. Cancer wasn't simply happening to the inside of my body, but it was also changing my outward appearance. Now others could physically see cancer taking its toll.

"When you're ready to cry and talk about it, I'm here," a friend said to me one day. Not long after that, someone else told me, "You make chemo look fun; you never seem to have a bad day." Those words hurt. The one way I didn't want to respond in this journey was in pride or hypocrisy. *God, I never once wanted to make this look fake—it really has been Your grace and strength holding me together and pulling me through. How can I be in denial about this diagnosis? I'm throwing* up; *I have mouth sores; I lost my hair. This is real, and I'm not sure how I could deny that I have cancer. God, I need Your grace and strength to know how to respond when others don't know how to respond.*

His answer? Funny moments. Something about this wild ride needed occasional laughter. God's peace enabled me to discover the humor. These moments were an invitation to a deeper intimacy with Him. He knew me. He knew what would make me laugh and even how to draw others into something painful like cancer.

CALL ME CRAZY

I approached the grocery store checkout line with my basket full of chemo-staples: my favorite chips, Sprite, applesauce, and a frozen pizza to celebrate when I began to feel good again.

As I unloaded my groceries onto the conveyor belt, I could see the cashier eyeing my hat.

God, what do I say? She sees I'm bald. How do You want to bring her a smile today?

"Hi, did you find everything OK?" she asked.

"Yep," I responded.

Beep. Beep. Beep. The items passed over the scanner and onto the bagger at the end of the lane.

"Your total is $25.68," she said as she looked at me.

I handed her a twenty and a ten and then waited for the change.

The computer began to print out my receipt along with coupons for my next shopping trip. The cashier eyed the receipt to tell me how much I had saved, as well as the coupons. Her eyes glanced uncomfortably at the coupon and then back up at me.

"You saved $2.75 today... Here is a coupon for next time."

I glanced down at the coupon: "Healthier color & softer hair in 10 minutes. $5 off any two boxes of Natural Instincts hair color." *God, that is perfect!*

"This could come in handy!" I said as I smiled at the cashier.

The awkward moment shattered into giggles. And I continued to chuckle as I headed toward the door.

A few weeks later, my friend and former Colorado roommate, Tra'Cee, came to Indiana to visit and together we decided to create some humor.

"Krish, I can't believe these made it through airport security," she laughed as she dug into the front pocket of her suitcase. "Here. Look at these!" she exclaimed.

In her hands were two wigs. One brunette and the other blonde. Both curly and both mullets.

"Oh. My. Word." I said as I grabbed the blonde one to try on. "How does this look?"

"Perfect!"

"I have to wear this out somewhere and see what kind of response I get."

That night I took Tra'Cee to youth group. She had heard me talk about the new friends I had met, Tammy and Denise, and the teens I had been serving.

Before we got out of the car, I looked around to see if anyone was watching. We had arrived early enough for the youth leaders' meeting that I could slip on the brunette wig, positioning it in such a way to make it look as if I was serious about this new look.

I walked in as confidently and casually as I could. It was hard to keep a straight face.

Cody, the youth pastor, headed our direction. "Hi…" he paused for a moment and then realized who I was.

"Cody, this is my friend, Tra'Cee, visiting from Colorado," I said.

"Hi, Tra'Cee, nice to meet you," he responded, trying to keep a straight face while glancing back at my wig. I could tell he struggled to know if it was appropriate to laugh.

Tra'Cee shook his hand, and we headed into a side room for a leaders meeting.

Cody explained the topic for the evening and offered ways in which we could reach out to the students who attended. While he talked, we could see leaders come in late and do a double take whenever they glanced my direction. Whispers increased. I'm guessing they were asking the person beside them if I was serious about this hairstyle.

Finally, Tammy and Denise walked in the room. They knew me really well by this time and tried to hold back their laughter as Cody finished talking. My hair was causing a lot of disruption.

We huddled up to pray. Cody made eye contact with me before he closed his eyes, "God, thank You for Krishana's hair!"

I couldn't hold my laughter in any longer. That's when everyone lost it. And it took us a few minutes to get serious enough to pray.

SO MANY HATS

Actually, I didn't choose to wear a wig at all. The summertime heat didn't make a wig practical for me. Instead, I wore hats and bandanas. Along with many cards from all over the U.S. and a few overseas, a lot people sent me hats. I had such an assortment that I wasn't sure what to do with them all.

Then I got an idea.

I opened the front door to my parents' house as Tammy pulled her red SUV into my driveway. Her daughter, Danielle, opened the front passenger door and slipped out of the vehicle with a backpack in hand. She had just finished her school day and had come to help me with a photo project for my blog.

"Hi, Danielle. Thanks for coming over," I said as I stood on the front porch.

"What time do you think you'll be finished?" I could hear Tammy asking from the driver's side.

Danielle looked my direction.

"Oh just give us an hour, if that works for you," I responded.

Danielle and I walked into the house where I had twenty-five hats laid out across the living room floor.

"So, I have been gifted many hats and bandanas," I explained to her. "My friends and family who don't live around here have said they would like to see photos of me in these hats. I'd like you to take photos of me in these different hats. Then I'm going to post the photos online and let my blog readers vote for the one they like the best."

"OK, sounds good."

I pulled out my digital camera and showed Danielle how to operate it.

"Got it?" I asked.

"I think so." Quiet at first, Danielle began to warm up as we continued the photos in my backyard. I goofed around, acting like a supermodel, fully knowing how crazy I looked with a puffy face and no hair. Another opportunity to laugh as Danielle captured my silliness.

"What if I place all of these hats around me in a circle and then toss a few of them up in the air? Do you think you could capture them mid-air?" I asked.

"I can try," she responded.

If there is anything I learned from youth ministry through the years, it's that any opportunity I can get to bring a high school student into a project I'm working on, it's best to take it. I may not be in Vienna connecting with teens, but I could still be in southern Indiana investing in lives.

I looked at the living room clock. "We have a few more minutes before your mom gets here," I said. "Would you show me your pictures from your recent missions trip to the Dominican Republic?"

"Sure!" she pulled out her laptop and began to go through the photos describing the work, the people and her favorite memories. I resonated with her excitement. The joy of reaching others in another part of the world and seeing God work through their lives.

This was another way God reminded me that He was in every moment. I simply had to look for Him. And it was easier to find Him in that present moment when I wasn't obsessed with my next move.

A BUMPY RIDE

While God was teaching me about belly laughs, he was also teaching me about tears. Chemo number four had arrived, and since my parents had already taken so many days off of work, Tammy accompanied me to my appointment. She had become a regular at our house. She often brought over meals, and when I felt well, she would pick me up for an "adventure" even if that meant simply driving around town or having lunch at a park. Usually our time together was lighthearted. Today was different.

Before Tammy arrived, I gathered my snacks, movies, and medical binder. I glanced at my day planner to reassure myself of the appointment time. The words *Move to Austria* were written in bold, blue ink. My deadline had arrived to raise the rest of my financial support. But today I wasn't going to Austria; I was going to chemo.

Tammy rang the doorbell. "Are you ready?" she asked.

"I guess," I reluctantly responded. My heart was heavy as I carried my chemo-day supply bag to her car. Tears were bottled up inside me. But I wasn't comfortable sharing my tears with other people. Right now, I only shared my tears with Jesus. *Deep breath, Krishana.* These tears would have to wait.

As Tammy drove down the interstate, I let the radio fill the silence in the car. Somehow she knew I needed to be quiet.

Jesus, I want to go back home, close the bathroom door, and cry. Why do I have to go to chemo? Why am I not on a plane headed to Austria? You know every tear I've cried on this journey—which hasn't always been adrenaline rushes with breathtaking views. Some days it's been more like a tandem-bike climb in low gear. Our cadence is slow, and the journey is bumpy. I'm the one in the back, so, of course, I don't see where we're going. Everything around me tells me to jump off and get moving on my own. But everything in me says, "Hold on; you don't know what's around the bend." Something is different about this trail—and about us. I thought I knew what "us" looked like, but I guess it's not like the "riding a bike" I always thought I knew. Teach me how to ride with You, Jesus.

As we pulled into the parking lot of the cancer treatment center, I could picture the bold, blue words from my day planner, the screaming reminder that all the pieces of my life had been thrown in the air.

Deep breaths, Krishana.

SEEING THE PUZZLE

The teen girls were still holding their puzzle pieces. I asked them to pick a characteristic of God that spoke truth to combat one of their biggest fears or anxieties and write it on their puzzle pieces.

"Just as I handed my cancer to God, each of us can hand Him whatever puzzle piece we hold because ultimately He's in control. Whatever we're going through right now is just one small piece in the big puzzle of our lives. Somehow all of these pieces will come together for His glory."

"OK, let's put this puzzle together."

The girls looked at me a bit confused.

"I promise these puzzle pieces fit together." I said.

As they worked together, the puzzle started to spell out P-E-A-C-E. In addition to the word *peace*, the puzzle was covered with attributes of God they had written on their individual pieces.

In that moment, I wondered what other pieces God would be putting into my life. I'd given up trying to figure it out.

CHAPTER 9

Re: Mission

How beautiful on the mountains are the feet of the messenger who brings good news,

the good news of peace and salvation the news that the God of Israel reigns! (Isaiah 52:7 NLT).

"Call your dad!" my mom gleefully shouted.

It was a bright sunny day in the middle of June, and the temps were rising. My mom and I had just left the oncology office. We had been up since 5:30 a.m. so I could travel to Louisville for a PET scan. It had been three months and five chemo treatments since my last scan.

While Nurse Kim administered a shot to boost my immune system, she told me stories about her adventures with her two dogs. I mustered up the courage for my question.

"Do you know if my PET scan results are in?" I asked, trying to hold back my anticipation and nervousness. I hadn't even completed all six treatments. *God, do I even want to know the results?*

"I'm not sure, but I'll go check," she responded.

Last week, I had attended a Cancer Walk to raise funds and awareness for the need for a cure. They had what they called a Cancer Survivor's Lap. Each cancer survivor walked up to the mic, and the coordinator asked how long he or she had been in remission. As I heard these men and women say ten, twenty, or even thirty years, I didn't even know if the cancer in my body had been gone for ten minutes. I didn't know if I was a survivor yet, but I walked up to the mic. "I'm not in remission quite yet," I stated. The lady gave me a big hug and cheered me on.

What if today I could finally say, I'm a survivor?

I could hear quick footsteps coming toward our room. Nurse Kim entered beaming and immediately handed me a copy of the PET scan report. With tears in her eyes, she said, "There are no abnormalities. The scan is clear!" My mom and I sat there for a moment. Then we leapt out of our seats and hugged each other and hugged Kim. She felt just as much a part of our family in this moment. Kim went over final instructions and scheduling my next appointment, but she knew we wanted to get out the door to celebrate. I gripped tightly to the copy of the PET scan report.

After Mom and I climbed into the car, I called my dad, who was still finishing up his workday as a sixth grade teacher. He finally answered.

"Dad, I had a clear PET scan! The cancer is gone!" I exclaimed.

"Wow! That's great!" he responded. I could almost hear him smiling over the phone, one of those smiles so big that he couldn't keep his eyes open. "Where should we celebrate?"

"Doesn't matter to me as long as it includes a good steak!"

"Perfect!"

"I'll talk to ya later, Dad. See you soon."

After signing off, I began to go down the list and share the good news with the many people who had faithfully prayed for me. When my diagnosis had come, I had so many people who came alongside me. The other youth leaders I served with at church had become like family, and they showed themselves as such when crisis hit my life. It was strange how I went from dreading my move to Indiana to developing some incredible friendships. *God, You brought me to Indiana before I was diagnosed so these friendships could start to grow. You knew I would need these people. Thank You for these friends I call family.*

My phone continued to ding as people responded to my calls and text messages. For the last six months, I had been a cancer patient; now I was a survivor.

God, thank You for the peace You gave me through all of this. Thank You for pedaling when I couldn't. Thank You for Your overwhelming love and the ways You've given me so many sweet blessings. I realize this could come back. But I trust You. There is no point in worrying when everything is in Your hands. Whatever I get to be a part of in the days to come, I know that all You have your hands in will be amazing. Thank You that You require dependence.

WHERE DO I BEGIN?

Remission is defined as a state or period during which something is remitted or to be free from. In my case, the cancer was remitted. However, I was disappointed to learn that this didn't mean I'd also be free from chemo treatments. I would need a maintenance chemo treatment every three months for two years to keep this treatable, but incurable, cancer at bay.

So when you tell a driven young woman that her cancer obstacle is gone, her most natural reaction is to strive with all her might to get done what she needs to make "Austria happen." Now, though, I realized that I wasn't the same Krishana any longer. The Krishana who used to squeeze in an international trip alongside missionary training school with one day in Indiana to do laundry, go to the doctor, get my oil changed and repack, couldn't operate at that speed or with that energy like she used to.

Now that I was on the other side of cancer, it would have been so easy for me to say, *OK God, I have it from here; I can take it the rest of the way.*

As I talked to God about these new challenges and my deep desire to move to Austria, I didn't get the impression that He wanted me to stay in Indiana. First Peter 5:7 resounded in my heart, "Give all your worries and cares to God, for he cares about you" (NLT). *Wow. You want me to be carefree? Really, God?* He was leading me forward. And my excitement grew.

Now, I had to relearn how to pedal-out this tandem living journey. My spiritual legs had become weak. My daily struggles and insecurities resurfaced as rough terrain on a bike path. I felt so inadequate and even somewhat disconnected from all those desires that had propelled me toward Austria in the first place. *What do I really know about youth ministry? How could I even begin to think I could connect with Austrians? How could I make a difference in this new mission?*

REDEFINED

I stared at the word *remission.* I love words, but this word, *remission,* wasn't doing anything for me. It seemed so technical. I began to play with the word.

Re: reminded me of the notation you receive in the subject line when someone replies to your email. *Hmm, a response. A response to what, God?* As I stared at the word longer, something stirred within my heart. Remission was more than having a clear scan. I had a new mission. A *re:mission* to make God famous around the world. He obviously doesn't need me to make Him famous, yet He somehow wanted to use me and my story.

These last few months were some of the most faith-stretching yet faith-filled months of my life. I was learning to do this life in tandem: God steering and me going along for the ride. Is it strange that trusting Him with this new mission felt bigger than trusting Him with cancer? Going along for the ride was a lot easier than trying to pedal-out what He had taught me. It takes more energy to keep your feet in sync with His cadence than those moments of propping them up on the bike frame while He does all the pedaling. He still gave me His strength, but I needed even more of it because this pedaling thing took more than I had to offer.

He let me see a bit of what He was up to through how people described what they had seen in my life. People told me how my response to cancer and how I lived in those moments had inspired them. Yet I wasn't *doing* anything. I was simply seeking God in the midst of seeking survival.

PREPARING FOR THE MISSION AHEAD

Even before my remission, Jim, the GEM Austria director, had emailed me. My resident permit had finally been approved (third time's a charm!), and I needed to go to Austria to retrieve it. I had six months to fulfill this task, or I would lose my permit and have to start all over. Time was running out.

Only two days after landing in Vienna, Jim and I headed to the Austrian government building where they were holding my resident permit.

As he found a place on the city street to park, I smiled. *All while I was having biopsies, chemo treatment, and oncology appointments, God, You were putting together the necessary pieces for a resident permit to live in Vienna. Your timing is perfect.*

Jim pulled out prepaid parking passes and put them on the dash of the car. The hope was that we would be finished in under two hours. I opened my door, and the wind came rushing into the car, swept the parking passes, and rushed right back out.

"Oh no!" I exclaimed.

Jim froze. Without the parking passes, he could receive a huge fine.

I responded the only way I knew how, I ran. The parking passes landed in the street. I grabbed one, but the other one got away, the wind picked it up again and took it farther down the street. I kept running. Finally, the second parking pass landed, and I quickly stomped on it before the wind carried it again. I felt as if I had run three miles; it was only 300 feet. I caught my breath and tried to compose myself.

When we finally got called into an office, Jim did all the talking. I could pick up a few words here and there, but I hadn't been immersed in the German language for eleven months. The woman handed me a pinkish card with my picture on it. I had another piece to the puzzle. The only thing left was the remaining $500 of monthly support.

Besides being excited about my resident permit, I couldn't wait to see Waltraude. After living with her for five weeks, we had communicated with each other via email for nine months. When she heard about my cancer diagnosis, she wrote (in German, of course!):

Hello Krishana, I think of you often and am sad that you are not doing well. I am praying for you and wisdom for your doctors.

Tonight, Waltraude had coordinated a group of ladies who knew me to dine in an Austrian restaurant and eat goose. In Vienna, at certain times of the year family-owned restaurants provided customers with their best wine and authentic cuisine.

As I turned onto Waltraude's street, so many memories flooded my heart. Cramming my luggage in the small elevator, ringing Waltraude's doorbell accidentally, and trying to make the perfect cup of coffee. I walked this way every day before and after language school last January. I had no idea what was coming around the corner in my life. I didn't know it would be cancer. My heart beat faster as I approached the familiar apartment building.

Waltraude had pulled her car out onto the street so we could drive to the restaurant. As she got out of the car, she embraced me, kissed both of my cheeks, and started speaking German really fast. It didn't matter that every bit of German I had learned was gone in that moment. I couldn't stop smiling. Her words, while I didn't understand, were soothing to my soul. Now after months and months of prayer, she could see God's answer in person.

I became curious about my cancer story. Something about what I had been through seemed to create an invitation for a deeper relationship. I had only lived with Waltraude for five weeks, yet somehow our connection was so much stronger this time. *God, how are You planning to use what I've been through to grow relationships here? I'm watching.*

NOT ALONE

"Hi Krishana. It is wonderful to see you," Dawn greeted me as I entered the foyer to her house. My GEM team was having their monthly meeting while I was in town.

"It is great to see you too." I said, leaning toward her for a hug.

After taking off my shoes, I joined her and Jim in the living room and found a seat on the couch. Jim and I had arrived early to discuss a few questions Dawn had prepared. With her oncology background, Dawn brought up concerns I needed to think about as I transitioned to Austria and continued my cancer treatment: Who would be my oncologist? Who would go with me to my appointments and chemo treatments? How would I balance treatments and my language school requirements both for the Austrian government and GEM? What part of the city would I live in considering my health issues? She had thought about all the details. In my head, I was just thinking I needed to get back to Austria.

"Those are great questions, and I'm not sure I have answers to them, but they do bring up a lot of concerns. I realize I'm not your typical missionary," I said. "However, there has been no doubt in my mind about *still* coming, even after all that has happened."

"We want you to have the best transition here as possible," Dawn replied. "There are a lot of things to think about as a cancer survivor, let alone in a foreign culture."

My medical treatment would look different, but I didn't want my continued chemo treatments to stop me from coming. I had already experienced two maintenance chemo treatments, and they were manageable, not causing intense side effects like the initial six rounds of chemo. I wasn't giving up.

"I understand," I smiled. All the questions could have been overwhelming, but I actually greeted them with joy. I was thankful—Dawn truly understood what it meant to me to live here, and here we were, in Vienna, finally talking about this reality.

When the rest of the team arrived, we talked through a few details with the group. As the meeting came to a close, Jim shared his thoughts about me moving to Vienna in January.

"Who would've ever thought a few months ago that we'd be talking now about you coming. Your story is a powerful ministry, Krishana, and maybe there will be ways your story can be told as part of your ministry here. We don't know what this next part of the journey will be like, but we say yes to you coming."

Heads nodded as the rest of the team agreed.

"I can speak for my family," Eric said. "Christy and our girls, Kati and Elena, can't wait to have you here. I'm sure the girls already have a pancake breakfast planned for when you return."

I giggled. Eric, his wife, Christy, and their young daughters, Kati (eight years old) and Elena (two years old) had become a special part of my Vienna memories. Having been to Austria twice already to apply for my resident permit, I had gotten to know their family. The first time I spent an extended amount of time with them, I had breakfast at their house. Pancakes. From that point on, pancakes were our tradition. I couldn't wait to get back to Vienna and spend more time with them and their girls. *God, thank You for Your faithfulness in bringing certain people into my life at pivotal times. You even provided an oncology nurse on my team in Austria. That is something only You could design.*

A week after returning from Austria, I attended a Sunday night youth gathering at church. Even though I hoped it would only be a short time before I moved to Vienna, I wasn't going back to my old ways of being consumed with timing and planning, so I volunteered to be a small group leader with my dear friend Tammy for a gathering of senior high school girls. God could use me anywhere, and here was as good as Austria.

"Krishana!" a group of teen girls yelled as they ran toward me and smothered me with hugs.

"How was your trip to Austria?" Denise, Tammy's sister, asked as she walked toward the group.

"I finally got my resident permit. My photo is hilarious. Wanna see?" I asked. I pulled out the pink card, displaying my black-and-white profile picture with a dreadfully serious expression on my face.

"It doesn't even look like you!" she exclaimed.

"I know. I'm usually not that serious, huh?" I chuckled.

Despite the laughter and hugs, something serious was eating at me on the inside—I would have another PET scan the next day. A battle for my mind was underway. So after the youth event was over, I grabbed Tammy.

"I'm so nervous about tomorrow. What if the scan isn't clear?"

I feared the cancer coming back and again losing the opportunity to move to Austria. Yet I was also facing another fear: What would it look like to actually experience everything I had talked and dreamed about for almost six years? How would I say good-bye? How would friendships change if and when I was cleared to move to Vienna? Through the last nine months Tammy and I had become close friends as she helped me navigate these months with cancer.

God, good-byes hurt so much. I'm sad. I so want to go, and know I must go, and yet it's so hard. I fear losing all the beauty You brought me in this season and the community that came with it. I trust You with that.

Tammy grabbed my hand and pulled me toward a bench outside the youth room. Enough speculating, it was time to pray. As Tammy prayed, tears fell from my eyes.

Krishana, the beauty continues right here. It's time to share your tears with more than Me.

Two days later the PET scan was clear.

My final monthly support came in.

More than fifty storage containers were packed and labeled along with the furniture that would make up my future apartment. All of it was shipped in a huge overseas container marked for Austria.

My family and friends gathered at the airport on January 27—almost a year after I began to notice large knots on the sides of my neck. I had said good-bye to cancer. Now it was time to say good-bye to the familiar. I walked through airport security sobbing.

Time for another jump.

A new mission.

Re:mission.

CHAPTER 10

Gott aber kann viel mehr tun

[But God Can Do Much More]

Now to him who is able to do immeasurably more than all we ask or imagine,
according to his power that is at work within us... (Ephesians 3:20).

I used all of my strength to pull the big blue duffel bag off the conveyor without knocking over the people standing around me. I was exhausted but finally in Vienna.

Every day a new piece of my developing life in Vienna came together. I met new people at church. Purchased a bed to be delivered when I had an apartment. Enrolled for my first month back in German language school. I even attended my first-ever Austrian potluck at church.

Yet three things still needed to come together at the perfect time. One, I needed to find an apartment; I had been living in Jim and Lynette's basement. Two, my container with my packed items and furniture would hopefully arrive *after* I found an apartment. And three, it had almost been three months since I

117

had my last maintenance chemo treatment. I needed to find an oncologist and start my next treatment as soon as possible. Dawn became my main liaison in helping me transition. She understood the importance of timing in all three of these.

By the time I moved to Vienna, I had known Dawn for two years. We had stayed in contact via email, especially through the months I battled cancer, so it was easy to be myself with her. I had already asked her plenty of questions about cancer. Now, I could ask her seemingly silly questions about life in Vienna, like which trash items you could throw away and which you had to recycle. Or do they even have cheddar cheese here? We'd talk and laugh, and we easily lost track of time when we were together.

After scouring apartment listings, Dawn helped set up appointments and picked me up at Jim and Lynette's house to go apartment hunting. When I got in her car, it was almost as if I forgot I was in a foreign country. But our first attempts fell flat. Apartments were posted and quickly snatched.

Then came a notification from the shipping company that my container would arrive soon—as soon as the following week.

"How long can I wait before I give you my apartment address?" I asked, somewhat panicked. If I had to cancel my container delivery, there would be more money involved. Initially, they had said the container could take six to eight weeks to arrive in Vienna, but they were early. We were nearing the four-to five-week mark.

"We need the address as soon as possible Ms. Kraft," the Austrian lady on the other end of the phone responded. It was Tuesday. I didn't have an apartment yet. We were leaving on our GEM Austria team retreat on Thursday afternoon.

God, if You're planning on showing up big *right about now, then Your* big *debut is coming—I'm watching.*

Wednesday. Dawn found out about an apartment that we would view Thursday morning at 10 a.m., hours before leaving on the retreat.

Thursday. Dawn and I walked through the apartment. It was close to public transportation (since I didn't have a car), on a side of town where I could easily connect with the teens who attended the Austrian church where I'd be serving, and it was the perfect size for the items I had already shipped to Vienna.

We kept looking at each other wondering why this apartment was still available. After many questions directed at the agent—this space became my new Vienna home.

I had a couple of hours before the team retreat, and I needed to get my cash deposit for the apartment while the bank was still open. I was only allowed to withdraw a limited amount of cash from the ATM at a time, and with the weekend and upcoming holiday, the bank lobby would be closed.

Dawn drove me back to Jim and Lynette's house. I swung open the front door and immediately saw Lynette sitting on the couch reading a book.

I quickly gasped, "I found an apartment!" as I ran down the steps and into the basement.

I grabbed my passport, resident permit, and banking information to secure the apartment and ran back up the stairs.

"I'll tell you all about it when I get back!" I shouted and ran out the door. Thankfully, public transportation had helped me gain a little more stamina to move quickly.

I had my new address. My container arrived about a week later. And even before I settled into my apartment, God had provided an oncologist. Number three—check.

God, You are the Creator of the Universe, and yet You care about the details of my life? I am blown away by Your provision. I know everything won't always be this easy. I know there will be many tough times. But You've continued to allow so many good things fall into place since I stepped foot into this country. Thank You! It's exciting to be here. Your personal love for me has shown up in these tandem-living moments. Here I am free falling, waiting for You to pull the 'chute. And You do. You show up. At just the right time.

THIS FEELS LIKE HOME

The best part about having an apartment was inviting people over—friends from language school, teammates from GEM, or teen girls from church. *Einladungen* (invitations) are an important gesture in Austria, so I printed a handful for a girls' night including pizza, games, and a movie and handed them out at church.

One by one, the doorbell rang and each time a teen girl would arrive with a smile on her face. Each would take off her shoes and hand me a box of chocolates, another Austrian custom when invited to someone's house for dinner. My plan was to speak as much German as I could, but after an hour of attempts, I gave in to conversing in English. *This is definitely not following my plan of using German, but I'll go with it.*

"Have you ever played the card game Dutch Blitz?" I asked as we sat around my dining room table.

They all shook their heads no and looked at me with curiosity. As I began to explain the game and show them what to do, they started whispering in German to one another.

"This game is like Ligretto," one of them said. "A game we play here in Austria."

I smiled. *God, how cool that this game is something these girls connect with.* For me, this game has sweet memories, competing against Tammy and her three kids, accompanied by a lot of shouting and laughing.

As the girls and I began to play, I started to get louder, "Hey! I was going to put my card there!"

They laughed. They weren't used to me being so vocal. At church I was usually quiet because I lacked the language skills to have much of a conversation after a few basic questions. Before I knew it, they were trying to outdo each other with their own version of "smack talk."

God, this is what I always imagined. Teen girls enjoying time in my Vienna apartment, laughing and eating pizza. Thank You!

The teen girls from church weren't my only guests. Eric and Christy's daughters, Kati and Elena were also frequent visitors. Not long after my arrival, Christy faced serious burnout, impacting her on many levels—physical, spiritual, emotional, mental. She had to bow out of her ministry obligations, as well as rely on Eric for their day-to-day routine, taking that time to rest and get better. I missed her. Yet having their girls over to my apartment was a win-win for all of us.

Back in Indiana, I had often created theme-night sleepovers for my nephew, such as Superhero Night with costumes, and superhero foods, desserts, and activities. Now I had two "nieces" to love on in Vienna, creating the same opportunities, such as Princess Night.

Kati, a brunette and vibrant eight-year-old, full of life and ready to run and play on any playground, was the first of the two girls to spend the night at my place. Elena, her two-year-old sister who wanted to wear a dress regardless of the temperature outside, joined the fun once she was potty-trained.

"Are you ready for tonight's theme?" I asked the girls as we walked into the entryway of my apartment.

"Yes!" Kati shouted.

"Yes!" Elena quickly parroted.

The three of us sat down on the rug just inside my front door.

"OK, well tonight's theme is Mystery Night," I told them. "And I am sending you on a scavenger hunt all around my apartment."

"Oh fun!" Kati shouted, standing up ready to begin.

Elena quickly stood up too, not knowing what a scavenger hunt meant, but if Kati was excited, then Elena knew she would be too.

I handed Kati the first clue.

"Kati, make sure you read it out loud so Elena can be a part of the hunt."

Kati and Elena hurried from room to room in my tiny one-bedroom place, finding clues in the microwave or taped under the dining table. Their giggles filled the space, which was usually quiet most days. Their last clue took them to the refrigerator where I had hidden chocolate candy.

As bedtime approached, I prepared the full-size air mattress with sheets and blankets, all of it fitting snugly between my dresser and bed. The girls, still a bit wired from Mystery Night, got under the covers. I handed Kati my headlamp so she could read before going to sleep.

"Good night, Kati and Elena," I said as I bent down to give them hugs. I stood up, turned off the light, and looked at my clock—nine p.m.; I knew the girls would be up with the sun, ready for pancakes. *I had better get to sleep!*

"Good night," they responded. I could almost hear the smiles on their faces.

What a great night, God. Thank You for the opportunity to create something special for these two! Sure, I'm tired, but look at what You provided tonight. Elena is asleep, and we even forgot to give her the bottle she usually takes before bed. Thank You that they feel comfortable and at home with me.

ICH HATTE KREBS (I HAD CANCER)

Christmastime is magical in Vienna. The city center is draped in sparkling white lights, resembling chandeliers hanging over the cobblestone streets. The Chriskindlmärkte (Christmas markets) offer aromas of roasted chestnuts and fried potatoes and rows of market vendors in little wooden booths that look like small American storage sheds. The atmosphere is more than enough invitation to come and sip hot drinks while standing around bistro tables enjoying company and conversation.

Two women in their twenties from church, Karin and Bianca, invited me to join them at the market located in front of the Karlskirche (Church of St. Charles). They had known each other for about a year, and we hit it off after a couple of laughter-filled conversations at church. With multiple market locations throughout the city, this was one of their favorites. Bianca and her husband had recently started leading the youth group at church.

I had heard it could take many years to develop meaningful friendships in Austria. Even though I'm not one to function on a casual level for very long, I didn't have the German language skills to converse on a deep level. I had asked

God on many occasions if I'd even have close friendships in Austria.

"Raclette Brot?" I asked pointing to a vendor sign.

"Das ist Käse mit Brot. Raclette kommt aus der Schweiz," Karin explained.

"Ah-so," I responded, nodding to her explanation of the hot bread and cheese combination from Switzerland. "Ist das lecker [Does it taste good]?"

"Ja!" Karin's eyes lit up. Many times, Karin's German was easy to understand because her face told the story.

Bianca and I laughed as Karin described the tastiness.

I ordered Raclette Brot, and we huddled around a small standing table. They were patient with my German language skills, and when it came to matters of the heart, they allowed me to share in English when I needed to.

Our friendship developed from moments of laughter to moments of transparency. On different occasions, as I began to tell them pieces of my cancer story, my vulnerability opened a door to a deeper friendship. Surprisingly, these two women were becoming dear friends.

"Ich hatte Krebs und das war schwierig... (I had cancer and it was difficult...)," is always where I would begin. I'd pick out a few German words such as *Friede* [peace] and *Freude* [joy] to express the gifts God gave me intermingled with English for what I couldn't describe in German.

Both women responded with empathy and grace. Then they would open up. Their stories would start with, "Manchmal, habe ich auch Schwierigkeiten... [Sometimes I also have difficulties...]."

God, I can't wait until heaven, when I get to share in conversation with these two without a single barrier. Help them to know how deeply I care about them.

Only God could use something like my cancer story to lead to unexpected relationships, even when the language and culture obstacles felt so big. My story was its own Einladung (invitation) to this tandem-living journey with God.

CHAPTER 11

Bis morgen

[Until Tomorrow]

Don't brag about tomorrow, since you don't know what

the day will bring (Proverbs 27:1 NLT).

Within my first month of living in Vienna, Dr. T agreed to meet with me. He was a Vienna oncologist specializing in blood cancers, such as Follicular lymphoma, and I had received his name and contact information on recommendation. In an email I had mentioned my diagnosis, the treatment I had received, and that I would need a maintenance chemo treatment as soon as possible.

Dawn and I had taken two U-bahns and a Straßenbahn [streetcar] to finally end up in front of the building where Dr. T's office was located. We both glanced at each other, wondering what the experience would be like. We had heard stories about the medical culture in Vienna. Typically, you didn't ask questions of doctors; you simply did what they told you to do. Anything less was disrespectful. I wasn't sure how it would feel to have a doctor with whom I couldn't easily converse or ask questions. Dr. J had always been open to my concerns.

Dawn pushed the button on the outside of the building, the door buzzed, and we pushed it open. Just in front of the reception desk on the third floor stood a tall man in a long white coat. He glanced at each of us, trying to pinpoint who was the potential patient.

I walked toward him.

"Hallo, mein Name ist Krishana Kraft," I said.

His eyes got big with surprise. He looked at Dawn, "In ihren Email, hat sie nicht gesagt, das sie so jung ist [In her email, she didn't say she was so young]," he responded.

"Mein Deutsch ist nicht so gut. Ich kann nicht immer verstehen [My German isn't great. I can't always understand]," I responded.

"Yes, of course," Dr. T replied. "I did not expect you to be so young," he repeated. "Krishana, tell me what brought you to Vienna?"

"I am here to mentor teens through the church I attend," I responded.

"I see. Do you enjoy living here?"

"Definitely! I have been waiting to move to Vienna for a long time," I said.

From that point on, Dr. T became fascinated with my case and agreed to take me on as his patient. He allowed me to be myself, never intimidating me. He always took the time to explain his plan of action and made sure I understood his reasoning.

Five months later, at one of my follow-up appointments, Dr. T noticed I had brought someone he hadn't met before. "Krishana, every time you come to see me, you bring a different friend," he remarked. "You must have a lot of friends."

I smiled. Dawn had gone to so many appointments with me that first month. Then every three months I would have a scan, a follow-up appointment, and a maintenance chemo treatment in a local Vienna hospital. Just about the time I became comfortable relying on Dawn, her oncology expertise, and companionship, her family then needed to relocate back to the States. Now I had to spread the wealth of scans, treatments, and appointments between GEM teammates and even a couple of language school friends.

"And you're always laughing," he noticed. I guess Dr. T wasn't used to cancer patients who laughed often.

My chemo treatment experience was different from what I had been familiar with in the U.S. Approximately twenty-five hospital beds sat side by side across a medium-sized room. Scattered here and there were also padded chairs with little side tables connected to them, much like a school desk.

Each person, whether in a bed or in a chair, was connected to an IV pump with whatever chemo concoction would fight their particular cancer. You could hear the pumps running and the alarms beeping when something needed to be adjusted. Even with all that was going on in that room and with all of those people, the atmosphere was silent and filled with heavy sadness. Some patients didn't have someone to help them through the day like I always did. Occasionally, I'd hear an older gentleman five beds down from me snoring. But besides the lady who always came by to offer the lunch menu, conversation and interaction was scarce.

I realized the honeymoon phase of my time in Vienna was dwindling. The jump into Vienna had been breathtaking, but now I was pedaling with God along a steep uphill. Living in Austria is quite different from vacationing in Austria. I had to complete the normal routines and tasks of a typical GEM missionary on top of keeping up with my medical treatment—from language school student to medical insurance liaison, which involved scanning receipts and making sure all of my maintenance chemo treatments were pre-certified.

I wanted to be one step ahead with the language phrases I would need, how I should get somewhere, how to culturally respond to others in certain situations and so on. Before long, I was constantly trying to anticipate what would happen next. I struggled with staying in rhythm of God's pedal cadence.

NOW THAT'S IMPRESSIVE

"Hallo, Krishana!" Waltraude greeted me, hugging me and kissing both cheeks. "Komm rein [Come in]."

"Hallo!" I smiled, as I bent down to take off my shoes.

Today was what was known as "game afternoon" at Waltraude's apartment. She held it once a month and invited me to come whenever I could. These same ladies, all mostly over age sixty, and I had dined on goose and celebrated when I came to pick up my resident permit last November. These afternoons with them created another opportunity to be immersed in German and continue building relationships.

The day started like every other time. First, we had coffee and a delicious dessert. Then we moved into game time—various card games or *Mensch ärgere Dich nicht,* the Austrian version of the board game *Parcheesi* or *Sorry.* While some aspects were considered casual, there was still a level of formality: using the nice dishes, following an order of events, and even though it is never said, making sure you compliment your host by staying longer than expected. After a couple hours of games, the host would offer a light dinner. This four- to six-hour event usually led to me thinking and dreaming in German.

When it was the dinner hour, I ate a little but started to feel nauseous. I looked at Vera, one of my GEM-Austria teammates, trying to show her by my expression that I was in pain. While Waltraude was busy in the kitchen, I leaned closer to Vera.

"I am not feeling well," I whispered. "I feel like I might throw up."

Vera's eyes got big for a moment.

"What should I say?" I asked. I didn't want to hurt Waltraude's feelings by leaving early. She always went above and beyond when it came to hospitality.

"Just be yourself and tell her you don't feel well," Vera replied.

I excused myself from the table and headed toward the kitchen. I explained to Waltraude my reason for leaving early. She quickly offered to drive me home. *How sweet,* I thought. *She always did want to take care of me.*

"Nein, danke [No, thank you]," I responded, not wanting to take her away from her other guests. I tried to construct the best German sentence I knew to explain that I thought I could make it home by myself. As I gathered my belongings and put on my shoes, I felt a sharp pain right under my ribs. I breathed deeply.

God, help me to get home.

After vomiting once that evening along with feeling the sharp pain around my ribs, I didn't think it was the stomach flu. I remembered one of my oncology nurses back home telling me over the phone that my PET scan showed I had gallstones. I hadn't felt a thing, and she didn't seem too concerned. I didn't think much more about it, until this moment.

I contacted Dr. T. After finding my gallbladder on the ultrasound screen, Dr. T remarked, "Krishana, you have two beautiful and impressive gallstones."

"Great!" I replied sarcastically.

"You will need to have your gallbladder removed within the next six months."

God, why is it that every time I seem to get moving and somewhat settled, things like "impressive gallstones" happen and I feel like I have to start all over?

This hadn't been the first time I had felt this way. Every time I had a maintenance treatment, I couldn't function at full capacity to keep up with language school, missions team responsibilities, or even social interactions. I learned this the hard way by trying to push myself too much with moving into a new apartment and jumping back into language school on top of my first-ever chemo treatment in Vienna—all within the course of a week. Sure, the before-cancer Krishana could've juggled a busy schedule that included a move to an overseas apartment but attempting such a feat now left me an exhausted, emotional mess.

I was only eight months into my time as a long-term missionary in Vienna and it was in my best interest to go back to the States for gallbladder surgery. Going home would be sweet in so many ways. I had stayed connected with my friends and family, regularly Skyping almost every week. Yet the trip back would only be confusing for my heart as it adjusted and embraced my new home in Austria. I dreamed of many years in Vienna, to be able to spout off German like I did English. To grow deep and rich friendships with Austrians and to see many youth come to know and experience and love my Jesus. Going home could make me more homesick when I returned to Vienna, and it would also interrupt my language and culture adjustment.

My teammates reminded me that one month in the U.S. for gallbladder surgery in the grand scheme of however long God had me in Austria was simply a blip in comparison.

CHAPTER 12

Gottes Rhythmus
(God's Rhythm)

Whether you turn to the right or to the left, your ears will hear a voice behind you,

saying, "This is the way; walk in it" (Isaiah 30:21).

I had almost completed a year in Austria, despite my impressive gallstones. And Christy had made headway in her recovery from burnout. She asked me to help her host Kati's nine-year-old birthday party. Sounded like fun to me.

A handful of girls piled into Christy's living room as I spread out a Twister mat.

"OK, girls, are you ready to have some fun?"

"Yes!" Some of them didn't know I typically had silly tricks up my sleeve.

I spun the Twister spinner. "Right foot on blue."

"Now, let's put your left hand on red."

These girls were smart. They had positioned themselves in such a way that they wouldn't get tangled or fall over. *OK, then, let's try something else,* I thought.

"Right elbow on yellow."

"Hey! That's not an option," one of the girls shouted.

"Oh, but this is Kati's special Twister game for her birthday," I responded, locking eyes and smiles with Kati, who looked like if she giggled enough she might knock down the whole group. She knew how silly I could be. Anytime we walked to the U-bahn station close to my apartment, I would tell her to listen closely for bird-like squawks I had heard before. I didn't know what they were, but I had come up with a story—just the same. "Kati, you know, wild turkeys live in the field next to this station," I'd say with a big smile. She would giggle.

"Now, put your *nose* on green."

The room erupted in belly laughs—one by one the girls tumbled to the ground.

Kati, Elena, and I had grown close. Each time I saw them, they already had a new idea for a theme night and couldn't wait for the next one.

As they headed to the States for a summer furlough, I already missed their giggles. However, my summer began to pick up speed. Attending a youth conference hosted in Vienna. Leading a small group of kids during an English camp through our church. Traveling to Germany for missionary training. Then off to London to volunteer at the 2012 Olympic Games.

"I know we had you signed up to serve bottled water or help the families of Olympic athletes get around London, however a more important need has come up," the ministry coordinator stated. "Are you willing to do something a little different?"

"Of course" I replied. *Sounds like an adventure!*

"Are you familiar with writing press releases or journalism?" she looked at me hesitantly.

"Actually, I have a degree in journalism," I responded with a smile.

"OK, wow! You will be perfect in helping in our media centre," she excitedly replied. "We need someone who can write press releases regarding events coordinated by our More Than Gold organization happening all across the London area."

"I'd be glad to help."

Unbelievable. How did I end up here? This is amazing, God! I'm willing to serve You here in whatever capacity, but I get to use my writing and creativity to serve You in London, at the Olympic Games. Thank You!

In the last year, God continued leading me along unexpected trails. I had already begun to dream what life would be like after language school. I had finally completed all of my formal language training and tests to maintain my Austrian resident permit. Now I had more freedom to continue my ongoing language learning. I could structure my own schedule. And I thrive in that environment—like having my own room and the ability to arrange the furniture however I like. Often, my parents caught me at age eleven trying to scoot my heavy clothes dresser across the room because I wanted to rearrange my bedroom. They would tell me, "Krishana, tell us when you want to move something and we'll help you." I would nod my head and think, *I really just want to do it myself.*

In September I would meet with Barbara, my German-language tutor twice a week. Barbara's gift of encouragement always left me feeling much better about my language skills than when I started our hour-long meeting. I would also volunteer to help with childcare at a moms' morning Bible study, where I hoped to share Bible lessons in German to toddlers and preschoolers. Stepping into more opportunities with teens was what excited me most. Now I could help Bianca and her husband lead the youth group at our church, another chance to do my own thing. And I liked it!

I had more control over what my daily schedule could look like, which was probably the only thing I could control. Stepping outside my apartment door could result in a variety of cultural scenarios that could leave me stressing, laughing, or crying by the end of the day. But looking back, I couldn't believe the steps I had taken outside of my own little comfy apartment and knew it was God's strength and courage that kept me moving.

UNCHARTED TRAILS

Late one Saturday night in August, I kept getting text messages from my mom about a young American woman named Rachel. She was also a missionary, but in Romania, and her dad was a pastor at a church in my hometown. The text messages were alarming: Rachel had an infection in her leg, and it may have to be amputated. She was on her way to Vienna for medical treatment. So many people who knew I lived there asked if I would connect with her.

That night I hardly slept.

I kept thinking and praying for Rachel, knowing somewhere in Vienna she was dealing with a medical emergency in a foreign country. I could empathize.

The next morning, I started my journey to the Vienna General Hospital known as the AKH, on the opposite side of town. I was so nervous. I didn't even know how I would find them in such a big hospital. I would have to use German. *God, help me!*

I approached the guy at the hospital information desk and fumbled the German question to ask where I could find Rachel and her family. Fortunately, he understood me enough to give me her room number and which floor.

Doctors and nurses were congregating outside of her door. They motioned for me to wait a few minutes. As I waited, I wondered what it would be like to step in that room having never met this family and dropping in unannounced.

Help me to have the words, Jesus. Help me to know what to do and how to respond.

Once the medical team exited, I knocked and peeked inside. I immediately saw Rachel's mom and introduced myself. "Hi, I'm Krishana Kraft. I'm a missionary here in Vienna and heard about your situation. I know you've never met me, but could I come in?"

With smiles, they welcomed me into the room. While Rachel was in a lot of pain, they had pumped her full of antibiotics to stop the spread of infection. She would need reconstructive surgery with skin grafts after the doctors removed as much of the infection as they could. No amputation. This would still be a long journey for Rachel, but I breathed a sigh of relief.

My mind started to go into brainstorming mode. I knew several things that would make this hospital stay much more enjoyable. New GEM-Austria teammates, Kimberly and her husband, Gregory, had arrived in Vienna about four months before and had extra cell phones they weren't using. I had magazines and an iPod with movies on it. So I spent the day gathering items and connecting the cell phones to an Austrian provider. Rachel's mom wasn't allowed to stay in the room overnight, so communication was important in case Rachel needed someone.

God, I had no idea that You would use me in this way—that being in Vienna and having experienced what it's like to be in a hospital here could help someone else. I can't believe I just went to the AKH not knowing what I'd find. Thank You for the courage You gave me. You continue to surprise me. Thank You for using me in the middle of all of my weaknesses.

I wondered what surprises He would have in store as I approached September and a brand new schedule. I could hardly wait.

CHAPTER 13

The Blue Plastic Bag

Why, you do not even know what will happen tomorrow. What is your life?
You are a mist that appears for a little while and then vanishes (James 4:14).

Only days after helping Rachel, I was preparing for my second-to-last maintenance chemo treatment. The final one would be in November. Then I would get my life back and only have to go to the doctor every six months rather than every two to three months.

I needed to pick up my scan results at the diagnostic imaging center connected to the mall. (I would joke that I could go have a CT scan and then stop by Cinnabon on my way home.) In Vienna, I had to pick up my scan results and take them to my doctor. Because most people travel on public transportation, they put these important documents in a blue bag you can easily carry. Walking around the mall, I'd see people with blue bags knowing they, too, had some sort of medical report to take to their doctors.

I picked up my blue bag and headed home.

When I got to my dining room table, I pulled out the documents and scanned the report. It was entirely in German, and I usually didn't understand all of the medical terminology. But I noticed it was much longer than before. I looked back at the previous scan results. These were different.

I went into this second-to-last maintenance treatment on edge. Dr. T was nowhere to be found. Another oncologist approached me and said she would administer the chemo that day, since Dr. T was on vacation. As she went back to her office to gather more information about my treatment, I followed her.

"Excuse me," I didn't bother starting a conversation in German. I needed English in this moment. "Since Dr. T isn't here, would you mind taking a look at this CT scan report and explain what it says?" I asked, holding the document out to her.

"Of course," she responded, gently taking the document from my hands.

At that point, I knew something wasn't right.

"There are some significant spots under your arms and in your abdomen," she responded and then paused. "I would prefer you to go over this with Dr. T. He will be back next week."

"OK, thank you," I responded politely, but inside I was screaming, *Next week?!*

God, I'm not excited about what this next step might mean, but I'm so thankful You are with me. I can't imagine going through full-blown chemo treatments here in Vienna. I can't imagine putting my team through that. I pray that every one of those enlarged lymph nodes would shrink back to normal size, and I wouldn't have to make those decisions. Holy Spirit, meet me right here.

He responded through a verse that came to mind: "They do not fear bad news; they confidently trust the LORD to care for them. They are confident and fearless and can face their foes triumphantly" (Psalm 112:7-8 NLT).

I texted my parents and a few close friends in the States about the recent scan. My phone chimed again and again as they responded.

God, they feel so far away! To be at home is to be *with You—regardless of location. Be home for me. Be my everything.*

He responded with Philippians 2:13, "For it is God who works in you to will and to act in order to fulfill his good purpose."

God, I've been wrestling with what it means to be called by You. Some will say, don't go unless you're called. But then who is to say whether it was Your will to call someone to a certain location for only a short amount of time? Would it be failure if someone were called and left after a few years rather than 50?

Joshua 1:5, "...*I* will not fail you or abandon you," (NLT, emphasis added).

RELIVING A BAD DREAM

A week was a long time to hold a single puzzle piece and not see the greater picture of what could be potentially cancerous spots in my body. It was a crazy-making place, although quite familiar. The kind that took me back to an apartment in nowhere, North Carolina, in the middle of February.

I tried hard not to jump to conclusions and resume my normal weekly activities, but I had already started playing out the scenarios in my head. *Could I even take a six-month medical leave? What does this mean?*

Many of my GEM-Austria teammates had been generous with their time in accompanying me to appointments or scans. They would even stay the night in my apartment to make sure I didn't have a bad reaction or side effect after a day of chemo. As a single woman, I needed their help, yet sometimes that was hard for me to admit. I still wanted to do things myself. Who would I call this time?

I dialed my new GEM teammate Kimberly. She and her family had been in Vienna for about four months; they had provided the cell phones for the Romanian missionary Rachel. When we had first met, Kimberly and I had immediately connected. She told me once with a chuckle, "Krishana, you know before we met, I read your blog. I knew I'd like you and hoped we'd be good friends." That made me smile.

"Hello, Kimberly. I know this is late notice, but are you available to go with me to my upcoming oncology appointment on Monday?" I asked.

I wished Tammy or Dawn could be there. I could hear Tammy in my head as I organized what I needed for this appointment and wrote down questions. She had prepared me well the first time, and I used those same tools during my time in Vienna. Then there was Dawn who had been there with me for every first moment of my continuing medical treatment in Vienna.

Fortunately, Kimberly agreed to go and I was thankful she was there. I needed someone else to listen to what Dr. T said in case my mind went in a million directions. She had her little notepad ready for every word that came from Dr. T's mouth.

"Krishana, you brought another friend," Dr. T immediately responded when we walked into his office.

I laughed. *OK, laughter is good.*

Kimberly introduced herself and then Dr. T motioned for us to take the two seats in front of his desk.

"Krishana, these spots under your arms and in your abdomen concern me," Dr. T said. "There are also spots closer to the surface in your lower back. I would like to do an ultrasound to see if there is a good place to biopsy. A PET scan and blood work will let me know how to proceed… and to see if this is again Follicular lymphoma. I know your oncologist in the U.S. has mentioned this before, but it may be time to consider a stem-cell transplant, a common procedure for those with your type of cancer. I know if we get to those stages you would want to be with your family. I understand that."

Kimberly was writing as fast as she could. All I could do was try to absorb the information.

Dr. T and I compared calendars and began to schedule appointments. My emotional walls were going up. I didn't have time to deal with all of the questions, I had to go here or there and find out what was going on in my body.

God this is like a bad dream I'm living all over again. I can't jump ahead too far because it's too overwhelming.

By the time I approached the middle of my week of tests and scans, I was physically, emotionally, and mentally spent. I kept telling myself, *Krishana, just keep going. Only two more days and then you'll have answers. Two more days and if you want, you can go back to the U.S.* I didn't want to do this by myself. I wanted the comfort of the familiar. I wanted someone to swoop in and take care of me like my parents and Tammy had done more than two years before.

Once again, Kimberly and I met Dr. T at the hospital. He pulled us into a side room where we could talk about the results. The cancer had returned. It was strange to think that this cancer was growing inside of my body all the while I had been running three to five miles along the Blue Danube. I didn't feel sick. I didn't look sick. Yet my body had betrayed me again.

"Dr. T, I can't take the next steps for my health here in Vienna. I need to go back to the States and have the help of my family," I responded. I knew this was the right move. And at that point, I'm not sure my body could handle the layers of stress by undergoing another test or treatment in Vienna.

Dr. T didn't say much, but he understood. "I will have the necessary medical information for you to take with you in a couple days."

"Thank you," I replied.

Kimberly and I walked slowly out of the hospital and down the many steps that took us to the city street. We got on the U-bahn and headed to Christy and Eric's apartment. They lived close to the hospital and recently returned from their furlough. They knew we were coming but were not prepared for the news we would have to share.

Just two days before, Christy had gone with me to a PET scan appointment. When we had arrived, the PET scan operator opened the door and told me I was an hour late to my appointment. This was not a good start to my morning. Plus I was hungry, and with hunger comes many emotions. I had fasted for the PET scan but discovered that they also wanted to take blood right then. I hadn't been aware that I'd also need to give blood that morning. *God, You know how weak I already feel. Please help me not to pass out.*

After completing the scan, I sat with Christy in the waiting area of the hospital basement. Suddenly, the PET scan operator came out. She looked alarmed. She kept pointing to my hands. German was flying every direction, and I was completely confused. Fortunately, Christy was a pro and understood the language much better than I did.

Christy looked at me to explain, "They said that your hands must have some of the radioactive sugar still on them."

The lady urged me in German to wash my hands. I ran into the restroom and washed my hands. My heart was pounding.

After coming out of the restroom, they took me over to a large metal machine that looked like it was from the 1950s. When they turned it on, it sounded like the static coming from a two-way Walkie Talkie. The whole situation was unnerving.

They began to scan my hands to detect for radioactive material. The team of people would urgently send someone upstairs to check the levels and then come back down. I was being held hostage until the situation was all clear.

When Christy and I finally got in the elevator to leave, my heart was still pounding and my mind spinning.

"Krishana, are you OK? That was a really stressful situation."

"I guess so," I had replied with much uncertainty. As the elevator opened, we headed down the long hall toward the main entrance. We couldn't have left that building fast enough. I knew I was ready to go home and cry.

It felt like I had been on the verge of tears for the last two weeks.

Kimberly knocked on Christy's door, as I waited beside her. *I wish I were here to play Twister,* I thought. Eric opened the door and welcomed me in. I took off my shoes and made my way in to find Christy. Kati and Elena were both gone for the morning.

"Dr. T says the cancer has returned," I said. I had heard Dr. T explain it again and again, but now the reality was actually coming out of my own mouth.

We stood there in silence.

"I need a hug," I finally said, breaking the quiet.

It was the first moment I had been able to reveal my feelings. All of this emotion came rushing out from behind the walls I had been putting up in the last few weeks.

I sensed God saying, *Krishana, you don't have to wait to be in the States before you feel comfortable to* be *you. There is home for you here. Look at what I've done and the community you have. Look at the beautiful views I see as we've journeyed together here in Austria.*

I cried and cried. It felt like the tears wouldn't stop. My friends embraced me and surrounded me. They prayed over me and together we asked, *Why God?*

But I wasn't alone.

WHISKED AWAY

I had a few moments before my ride to the Vienna airport would arrive at my apartment. On Friday I had found out the final diagnosis, and here it was Monday and I was going to fly back to the United States. In those last moments at the hospital to pick up my medical records, Christy said it almost looked as if Dr. T would cry as we bid farewell. *Did he wonder, too, if we would ever see each other again?*

Christy and Kimberly took over the details of getting me back to the U.S. as quickly as possible. Kimberly even pretended to be me on the phone with an airline agent to get me a flight. Christy contacted my landlord, explained the situation, and worked out the details for the next six months of my lease. Both Christy and Kimberly went through my closet and started laying out clothes for me to pack. It was amazing to think all of the tasks to do—in a foreign country and in less than forty-eight hours—forwarding my mail, organizing my monthly bills, going over my renter's insurance policy.

Besides dealing with the practical, my heart was torn. This had become home and I didn't want to leave. Instead of the quiet, I longed for Kati and Elena giggles for one last sleepover before I left.

While I waited for my ride, I took pictures with my phone of every room. There had been talk that if I couldn't come back, friends would pack up my apartment for me. I couldn't even imagine that. *God, what are You doing? Why is this being taken away from me? All I ever wanted to do is follow You, and I'm here. Now I have to leave? What do You expect of me? I don't even know which way is up.*

He whispered Micah 6:8: "He has shown you, O man, what is good. And what does the LORD require of you? To act justly and to love mercy and to walk humbly with your God."

I flipped to that verse in my Bible, and beside it I had written, "6-16-2010— clear scan." I wrote that down because I didn't want to forget His faithfulness to me. It's like He whispered to my heart, *Krishana, don't fear cancer. Fear Me. I will fight for you. I am always enough.*

With my two suitcases, this was one moment where walking out my front door meant more than just anticipating whatever would come my way in Vienna. I didn't know if I would ever come back.

CHAPTER 14

American Reprise

I sought the Lord, and he answered me; he delivered me from all my fears.

Those who look to him are radiant; their faces are never covered with shame (Psalm 34:4–5).

As I sat on a plane crossing the Atlantic, I replayed the conversation I had with Tammy the night before I left Vienna.

"She won?" I shouted over the phone.

"Yes," she nervously giggled.

"So they surprised her by just calling her?"

"No, she doesn't know yet…. Hold on, my boys are going outside. I can't tell you until they go outside."

Tammy had texted to tell me her daughter, Danielle, had been selected as a finalist as part of a new American Idol contest.

About a month prior, I had submitted Danielle's name and a video of her singing the national anthem at one of her high school volleyball games. (I had attended the game when I was home for gallbladder surgery.) This contest involved nominations for performing before the panel of Hollywood judges. This was a dream for Danielle, and she had been such an encouragement to me when I was first diagnosed with cancer. After my nomination submission, I had talked briefly with one of the American Idol producers but never heard anything more.

The American Idol producer contacted Tammy, since I lived overseas, and finally announced Danielle had been selected. As part of the upcoming season, they wanted to surprise Danielle with a ticket to audition in front of the judges without having to go through the lengthy selection process.

"I'm sick to my stomach. I wondered if I should tell you with all that you have going on right now. Danny (Tammy's husband) told me I had to tell you," Tammy continued. "I told the TV producer that you were coming home. And she screamed, 'What?!' She couldn't believe there was a possibility you could be a part of this surprise. You have plans to go to a Carrie Underwood concert and surprise Danielle with this news. So make sure you tell Dr. J to work your biopsy or treatment around this concert! They want to do interviews with us at some point before the concert."

"I think I'm going to throw up too. And I haven't had treatment yet!" I responded.

"Get ready for this: They are going to make her sing! Oh, Danny said, I'm supposed to say, 'She gets to sing!' When this lady calls back, they want to know three Carrie Underwood songs Danielle knows the words to," Tammy explained.

"She will get to meet Carrie Underwood!" I squealed. "How can I go to bed now?"

"How am I supposed to do anything now? We can't tell anybody!"

"At least we're in it together. I guess, I'm coming back with a bang!" I said.

"Hey, only the best for you!" she giggled.

CULTURE SHOCK IN AMERICA?

My mom, Tammy, and I walked into the oncology office. Connie, the receptionist who scheduled my appointments and handled so many details with my insurance, immediately smiled and said, "Hey, girl! How are you?" with a mixed expression of *I'm glad to see you but wish you didn't have to be here.*

Tears welled up in my eyes. *She knew who I was,* I thought to myself. These weren't tears about cancer relapse or about having to leave Austria. These were tears from missing what it was like to go to a medical appointment and be greeted by someone as friendly and kind as Connie.

After a little catching up, Dr. J began to share her insights from the documentation I had sent to Nurse Kim via email. When the cancer had returned, I knew she would be the fastest way to get an appointment with Dr. J.

Dr. J had a plan. Like she had in the past, she discussed my case with a panel of oncologists while I was still traveling to the U.S. and had our next step of action against this treatable, but incurable cancer.

As Dr. J shared the details about a new chemo recipe, I immediately asked, "Will I have to take steroids?" My body remembered the jittery-ness and days of trying to eat pills mashed into applesauce.

"No," Dr. J responded.

"I'm ready to give you a hug! What about these spots in my back? My oncologist in Vienna wanted to biopsy them. Is that something we need to do right now?" I asked.

"Can you show me where these spots are?"

As she began to examine my back, I explained more, "I thought they were knots from so much summer travel, like I needed a good massage."

"I believe these subcutaneous lesions have formed in your back because of the cancer growing in your body," she said. "Instead of biopsying them, let's use them as markers. We'll know the chemo is working if they disappear. Remember the knots you had in your neck? Same idea. The knots got smaller, even after the first chemo treatment."

"I see," I replied. "My oncologist in Vienna had also mentioned a stem-cell transplant. What are your thoughts on that?"

"Before we can address the long-term possibilities of treating this cancer, we have to get you healthy first," Dr. J stated.

I breathed a sigh of relief. A stem-cell transplant had always been a possibility, but I wasn't sure I could handle all of the emotions and details that went along with that type of a treatment.

For now, the chemo I would undergo would involve five rounds —a round of chemo every four weeks, starting the next week. I calculated in my head, *This would mean I would be away from Austria for at least five to six months.*

Pretty much overnight, my country/location, job description, and cultural environment had changed. I found it difficult to shift gears. Everything about this situation felt overwhelming. I constantly received questions like: When are you going back to Austria? When is your next chemo? Are you staying in the United States? Are you going back to Austria? What will you do next? Will you go back after you finish these chemo rounds?

An "I don't know" felt insufficient, but that's really all I had for an answer.

In just the short time I was back, I acted like I was on vacation in the States, piling in as much fun as I could within a short amount of time. Why? Because I knew the chemo cycle. One or two weeks of feeling awful, and then once I started feeling like myself and regained energy, the cycle would start all over again.

One Sunday night, I joined Tammy for youth group at my church where I had volunteered for a couple of years before I left for Austria. *God, I'm thankful to be here, but this isn't where I belong.*

Before heading home, I grabbed Tammy.

"All the questions—what do I do with all of them?" I asked with tears in my eyes.

"Krishana, not a lot of people are going to understand what a lonely place this can be," she responded. "We need to come up with a great response to all of these questions. But first, you need to remember that you're not on vacation and think about taking care of yourself. You need to cancel what you have tomorrow morning and sleep in!"

I wouldn't have the energy or the immune system to do fun activities or be with the people I enjoyed anyway. All of the fun I had now was allowing me to escape the heart-breaking situation I was in. I didn't want to deal with the pain, but I knew it was coming. I knew I needed to be still, even if I was fighting it. I feared both the answers and the silence to my questions.

DID I ASK FOR THIS?

I call it heart nausea. Physically I dealt with stomach nausea from chemo, so it was easy to relate what was happening on the inside to what I was experiencing on the outside. It was tough to grapple with disappointment, confusion, and just plain sadness about everything from having cancer, to leaving Austria in such a whirlwind, to feeling like I was nearing the finish line of chemo, to now starting all over, to not knowing where I belonged, to missing my sweet spot of youth ministry.

I wished I could take some of that anti-nausea medicine they gave me before chemo to aid my heart.

God, there is no doubt in my mind that I was supposed to go to Austria and be in Austria. But why so short? What are You doing? I was only there for eighteen months. I was at college longer. "God, what did You do in eighteen months?"

It was hard to know what I even wanted or was supposed to want or what God wanted me to want. I wanted to make the decision right then and move forward. *Come on God, am I staying in Austria or moving back to the U.S.?* Here I was again pedaling faster, ahead of the rhythm of His timing. My prayers of frustration didn't clearly lead me in any direction, except one day, and one chemo round at a time.

I had the tendency to forget I was a cancer patient. The only thing God was calling me to do was to trust Him with whatever the reasons and outcomes might be. He wasn't asking me to solve the mystery or connect the dots. I didn't need to know right then what the next few months held, much less the next few years.

ALL-AMERICAN GIRL

With little time for chemo recovery, *my* next move was on a plane headed to Oklahoma City with Tammy, her husband Danny, Danielle, and Tammy's sister, Denise. The anticipation of this night was the best distraction for my heart nausea.

Danielle had no clue. She thought this trip was about me and my cancer story, and that someone had gifted me these concert tickets and were doing a video about my cancer story. Everything from the car that picked us up at the airport to the cookies we received in our room, to the limo ride to the concert all had my name attached to them. It was quite believable that I was the "celebrity" in this situation.

During the middle of the concert, Carrie paused in between songs to introduce her good friend and American Idol judge, Randy Jackson.

"What's up, Sooners?" Randy yelled as he approached Carrie. He then went on to explain that tonight Oklahoma City had someone in their 14,000-person audience who had been nominated to audition for American Idol. "There's a girl named, Krishana, who has nominated Danielle..."

At that moment, Danielle turned toward me, with a look on her face that said, *Did they just say your name? Is that my Krishana?*

"Surprise!" I shouted.

Before Randy even finished saying her name, Danielle covered her face with her hands in shock and was then whisked away onto the stage.

"I bet she's not nervous at all," Carrie said to the audience.

"Danielle, meet Carrie Underwood," Randy began. "This is kind of a wow moment, right, Danielle?"

"Yes!" Danielle gasped. I could barely stand it; I was so nervous and so thankful I wasn't on that stage.

"I hear you're a big Carrie Underwood fan," Randy said. "Well, Carrie, this girl looks very All-American. Why don't you sing a little bit of 'All-American Girl' for us?"

"No pressure," Carrie jokingly said as she motioned toward the thousands who had come to see her concert.

"Just a little," Randy added.

Danielle giggled and asked where to stand.

Carrie leaned over and whispered the first couple of words, and Danielle took it from there. A few lines into the song and the audience began to clap along as Danielle continued to belt out the first verse. When Danielle nailed the chorus, Carrie began to clap her hands in approval above her head. Randy got ready to stop Danielle, but she kept singing. She had come that far in the song; she wasn't about to leave everyone hanging.

The audience erupted.

After Danielle left the stage, she gave me a hug. As hard as it was to be back in the U.S. and despite all of the yuck, I couldn't believe I got to see Danielle wow an audience with the gift God had given her.

It had been a fun twenty-four hours, but I was ready to be home. The nausea and exhaustion from the chemo had caught up with me, and I wanted my own bed. With Danielle's beautiful voice running on repeat in my head, I knew I was far from being an all-American girl. Austria had forever changed my life and my perspective. Now it was up to God to show me what to do next. After my next chemo, I'd have to make definitive decisions about whether I would go back to Austria with the chances for another relapse or stay put and pursue a stem-cell transplant.

CHAPTER 15

The Road to Good-bye

Oh, how great are God's riches and wisdom and knowledge! How impossible it is for us to understand his decisions and his ways! For everything comes from him and exists by his power and is intended for his glory. All glory to him forever! Amen (Romans 11:33, 36 NLT).

God, what do I have to look forward to now? I needed to get out of bed and start the day, but I didn't want to, considering it was 4:30 a.m. and still dark outside. I reached for the lamp beside my bed. The light made me squint my eyes.

I glanced around my room at all the notes written with permanent marker on my walls. They had been there for more than a year, and now that I had been home for almost six months, they seemed more like wallpaper. These were notes my mom and dad had orchestrated when I came home for gallbladder surgery. I had become accustomed to them and forgot to really absorb what they said:

"I'm so thankful for you, Krishana."

"I'm glad you're home."

"I'm praying for you."

"Don't forget that He who began a good work in you will complete it (Philippians 1:6)."

"I know God has many plans for you; your love for our Lord constantly amazes me."

I feel so loved through encouraging words, and I definitely felt that when I walked in my room during an unexpected trip home. The plan was to paint over the writing, but that hadn't happened yet.

Here I was again, an unexpected trip—*home.* Even after six months, this still didn't feel like home. I tried to create home again by rejoining my church. My first morning at a women's Bible study, the leader said we were going to cover the introduction and lesson one within the 1.5-hour timeframe. There wasn't time for questions. There wasn't time to even talk with the people at my table.

As we sped through Scriptures, I couldn't digest what was being dished out. I started to write side notes in my Bible study workbook, but after thirty minutes, I put down my pen. I couldn't keep up. My brain felt foggy. *Was the chemo doing this? Am I not used to this American pace?* The leader's words entered my mind like unexpected guests. Where were they supposed to sit down? There was already too much going on inside my head. *What was wrong with me?*

I missed the relational aspect of Austria. Something in their culture put priority on relationships over information. Anytime I would step foot in my church in Vienna, I was greeted multiple times. With the ladies I was closest to, that even involved kisses on either side of my face on both cheeks. I missed *that* home. I missed those relationships.

I wiped the sleep from my eyes and headed toward the shower. We would be leaving soon to meet with the transplant doctor and her team for the first time.

I want to stay in bed. Why can't my transplant doctor be in Louisville rather than two hours away? Have I made the right decision?

I had finally come to that crossroads, and I chose the stem-cell transplant.

The process of killing my immune system and receiving new cells required at least a four-week hospital stay. A stem-cell transplant would replace my unhealthy blood-forming cells with healthy ones. After settling into the hospital on arrival day, the next six days would involve chemotherapy—larger doses than I had ever taken. Some days chemo would last thirty minutes and others four hours. These doses would be large enough to obliterate my immune system. Then after six days, I would receive the new cells intravenously, much like a blood transfusion.

The cells could take approximately two to four weeks to find their way to the bone marrow and begin creating new white blood cells. In the meantime, without white blood cells, I wouldn't be able to fight infection. The common cold would be just as dangerous to me as pneumonia.

Until my white blood cell count steadily increased, I wouldn't know if the process was working and the cells were engrafting (making themselves at home). I would have to wait and see. There would be no exact date to go home.

After the hospital stay, recovery is approximately one to two years, depending on whether I chose to use my own cells or a donor's. That recovery time includes multiple weekly appointments, blood tests, scans and dealing with side effects, such as graft-versus-host disease (which is when your body rejects the new cells and attacks them, causing painful ailments such as skin rashes, liver disease, intestinal problems, etc.).

None of these options sounded inviting. I wanted to go back to bed and pull the covers over my head until the day cancer would simply go away.

An oyster sometimes pulls covers over its head—and for good reason. When something foreign enters its shell, it uses a substance called nacre to cover the intruder. This is a form of protection. While in the darkness, the intruder is transformed into something beautiful as it's covered by this protective substance. An average, natural pearl can take two or even three years to form this way.

It was as if I was sitting in an oyster and I could see its shells slowly closing around me. The darkness was growing.

Don't you see, Krishana. These aren't shells closing in around you. These are My Hands. "He has hidden me in the shadow of his hand. I am like a sharp arrow in his quiver" (Isaiah 49:2 NLT). Hands enclosed around me. Huge hands, the hands of our Creator and Redeemer, who I couldn't explain away or control. Too many times, I didn't understand His ways. I may not *feel* safe, but I knew He was good.

THE INTRUDER

Dr. J had always told me my cells had an attitude. Follicular lymphoma was more common for people over age sixty-five, and remission was usually five to ten years. However, in my case, I was only thirty when first diagnosed and my remission lasted fewer than two years.

She had explained the risks of the options in front of me. I could return to Austria and see how long my remission would last after the chemo regimen I had just finished. However, the lymphoma could come back in a different form, a form that may not be as treatable. Or I could take a risk of finding new cells that had a good chance of giving me life again, hoping the new cells would make themselves at home in my body. And hoping to get closer to a cure and a long-term remission.

As I headed toward the left fork in the road, I had to decide whether I would use my own cells or find a donor. The risk was even greater if I used a donor because it was unknown how my body would respond to foreign cells.

My cells with an attitude didn't recognize cancer and let it grow undetected, so it was hard for me to imagine how even after they removed some of my cells, get them all cleaned up and put them back that they wouldn't go back to their old habits. I have a tendency to go back to my old habits, so why wouldn't my cells? My body had betrayed me twice already. I leaned more toward the greater risk—an allogenic stem-cell transplant from a healthy donor.

FINAL DECISION

My brother, Kevin, who typically worked the night shift, slept in the back seat as we headed toward the transplant hospital. He was in tow, not only for support, but also in hopes that he would be my donor. They would give him a swab test and send it to the lab to see how many human leukocyte antigen (a protein found on most cells in your body) characteristics matched my own. The goal was to find a nine or a ten match out of the ten characteristics they looked for.

The nurse led me and my family down a hall to a large examination room. I already missed Connie, Nurse Kim, and even Dr. J. Here I was again in a new place. Yes, they spoke English, but this hospital wasn't familiar.

My transplant doctor entered with a stack of papers and a folder. She found the closest empty chair and pulled it up to join my family. Another woman, tall with dark hair and a dark complexion, followed her into the room. She shook my hand and introduced herself as my transplant coordinator. Her accent had a European sound to it. I smiled. I was desperate to connect with someone who knew more about my former home—the one where I still had an apartment and hoped to visit before God's Hands closed around me—isolation.

As the meeting began I pulled out my list of questions. While all of the medical questions were important in finalizing this decision, my biggest question was about taking an international trip. Dr. J and I went back and forth about it. She always saw me as a whole person and not just a patient, but this time the risk of being overseas not only with keeping the cancer at bay, but also with the timing of when the matching cells were available, caused her more hesitancy. However, she left it up to my transplant doctor.

I wanted to be in Europe for six weeks. It sounded as though I may get three weeks. But I still wanted to fight for four. Cancer had already taken so much I didn't want this trip to be destroyed too. It's like this tandem-ride with God had led me to these beautiful vineyards—and then cancer had doused them in gasoline and was ready to set them on fire. *All that You have planted—youth ministry, missions, Austria, living cross-culturally, adventure. What will I even have left, God?*

After working through my two pages of questions, waiting for my brother's swab results, and giving the transplant team plenty of my blood, I slumped back into the car with my tired family. My brother was now more alert and took over the drive back home. While this hospital didn't have the comforts of the familiar, this did appear to be the right direction.

HIS HANDS

March had arrived and no stem-cell match was on the horizon. My brother was only a twenty-five percent match.

God, I want a match, but I also fear finding one. Finding a match makes actually having the stem-cell transplant become reality. I'm so scared.

I continued to question my transplant doctor and coordinator about the timing and process of everything. The longer I waited after my last chemo treatment, the more chance I had that the cancer would return before a match became available. Dr. J said she wanted me to go into a stem-cell transplant healthy. Finally, after many conversations, I convinced them to let me go to Austria for a month.

My version of healthy included a chance to say good-bye. Once I began the transplant process, I wouldn't journey back to Austria for a very long time. Since Austria is a culture all about relationships, I knew I couldn't swoop in, get packed, and let my community in Vienna know how much they meant to me. If a game afternoon at Waltraude's was four to six hours, then saying good-bye needed more than a week.

Eric, Christy, and their two daughters picked me up at the airport.

"Are you ready for our next theme night?" I asked Kati and Elena.

"Yes!" they shouted. Now ages ten and four, they were growing up so fast.

"Well, we are going to have a spa night—with manicures, pedicures, facial masks, and even cucumbers for our eyes!"

"That sounds fun," Kati said.

"We just need to figure out which date will work the best," I said, looking toward Eric and Christy.

Why do I have to leave these precious girls? God, You have created so much here. It hurts my heart to think of not seeing them every week and listening to their stories and sharing adventures.

Almost as long as I had known them, they had known me with a cancer struggle. They had such tender hearts and had been faithful praying for me. Elena consistently prayed that my hair wouldn't fall out, and Kati even made a cake for me after learning about my cancer relapse.

Besides this family and others in my Vienna community who would help me pack, I wanted to bring friends from the U.S. with me to get a taste of what my life had been like in Austria, to see my apartment, meet my friends, and make memories that we could share in years to come. I wanted to connect them to the stories I had already told and would continue to tell.

I had asked a handful of friends to go with me and waited to see who would be available, if any. After church one morning, Tammy and her sister, Denise approached me.

"Tammy and I were wondering what we should pack for Austria?" Denise asked with a smile.

"You're coming?" I shouted. I jumped up and down and smothered them with hugs. While I would leave in March, they would join me in Vienna at the beginning of April, right after Easter.

ENGLISH!

"Waltraude, ich habe dich vermisst [I have missed you]," I smiled and hugged her as she welcomed me inside her apartment.

"Krishana, du schaut gut aus [you look good]," she responded. I imagine many people wonder what someone will look like after five chemo treatments.

As I walked into her apartment, I noticed the dining room table was covered with a tablecloth and all of the nice dishes had been set out. Yogurt parfaits were held in crystal stemmed glasses and positioned on top of the main plate. There were glasses for juice and mugs for coffee. Spoons for the yogurt and spoons for the soft-boiled eggs. I could smell the fresh bread that filled the small serving basket and noticed the plates of meats and cheeses that had been carefully arranged. This was a breakfast for queens.

Beside my place setting was a tiny gray bear wearing a crocheted sweater.

"Hast du gemacht [Did you make this]?" I asked Waltraude, pointing at the sweater. I chuckled inside; the game afternoon ladies had tried to teach me to crochet. After two hours, I had only completed two rows. They decided it wasn't for me and, next time, I could read to them in German while they crocheted. I'm not sure which would've been more difficult.

"Ja," she smiled, and then quickly motioning for me to sit down so we could eat. Waltraude wanted to give me something small that I could take with me to the hospital and be reminded that she was thinking of me and praying for me.

"Dankeschön, Waltraude." I smiled as I took my seat.

Time flew by and my calendar filled with coffee appointments, dinners with friends, and even some packing. By the time Tammy and Denise arrived, I was ready for help and for adventure. In between packing, we fit in an excursion to Salzburg, Austria, about three hours by train to the northwest of Vienna. We explored the city and were always on the hunt for hot coffee, delicious desserts, and chocolate-covered pretzels.

Whenever something was in question—where to go, what to do, or how to get somewhere—Tammy and Denise would look at me to figure it out in German. Or Denise would approach strangers and say, "English?" Denise got so good at asking this question that once we were back in Vienna, we decided to use it as a code for: "This situation is stressing me out! Help!"

On my last morning with my church, Waltraude had never hugged me so tightly. Before heading home to continue packing, my friends Lisa and Helga prayed with me. Tammy joined us, so Lisa offered to translate Helga's prayer. The mix of the German with the English translation was like a symphony.

God, this hurts so much. My heart aches to leave. I don't even know if I'm saying good-bye to these dear Austrians for now or forever.

Back at my apartment, a loud buzz came from my door. Two men had come to purchase my washer and dryer. I hadn't even had time to fix myself a sandwich. I welcomed the guys in the apartment and quickly realized they didn't speak any English. I used German as best I could, but I could feel my blood sugar plummeting.

When they realized I couldn't understand or respond to their questions, they decided to start anyway, first carrying the dryer down to the truck. I tried to hurry before them holding doors and making the heavy lifting and moving as easy as possible. However, that hungry anger began to build inside on top of the stress that I was feeling knowing I was losing time for packing. A container to take all of my stuff back to the United States would arrive the next day.

As the guys and I headed back upstairs, they started to see if they could unhook the washing machine. I ran into the kitchen where Tammy and Denise were making sandwiches.

"English!" I cried out in a loud whisper. Denise handed me a sandwich.

"Eat this," she quickly responded. She could tell I was about to lose it. Tammy immediately left the kitchen and began helping the two guys with the washing machine.

I sat in the kitchen. Tears filled my eyes. Before I knew it, this apartment would be empty, my furniture would be packed, I'd be back on a plane, and this entire trip would feel more like a dream.

After two bites, the doorbell interrupted my spiraling thoughts. I put down my plate and opened the door to find Eric, Christy and the girls there to say good-bye.

"Eric and Christy! I'm so glad to see you. Could you help me with this washing machine situation?" I desperately asked.

"We'll try," Eric said.

I introduced them to Eric and the three guys began to figure out a way to load the washer without leaking water through the building. The last two items on my must-sell list were finally gone.

I shut the door and took a deep breath. I found my sandwich as Eric, Christy, and I talked about items I still needed to get rid of. Before I knew it, I had greeted yet another good-bye. I hugged Kati and Elena tightly.

ANOTHER UPHILL CLIMB

Only days after Tammy, Denise, and I arrived back home, I received a call from my transplant coordinator.

"Krishana, we have found two matches. Both ten-out-of-ten matches."

"Oh wow!" My mind began spinning. Maybe it was the jet lag or maybe it was the reality of the situation. A match meant the transplant and the isolation would begin soon.

"We will confirm the details to see which match most closely fits with your current blood type," she said. There was always the potential that my blood type could change through this stem-cell transplant.

"Thank you," I responded.

Until then, I had quite a few tests to make sure my body was as ready as it could be for the chemo ahead. Deadly chemo. Chemo enough to kill my entire immune system.

It feels as though there will never again be a beautiful view. All we're doing, God, is pedaling and pedaling. And this hill is steep. Where is this journey leading? How will You show up?

"...I will never leave you nor forsake you," (Joshua 1:5).

I will not fail you, Krishana.

CHAPTER 16

Transplanted

"I know the Lord is always with me. I will not be shaken, for he is right beside me.

No wonder my heart is glad, and I rejoice. My body rests in safety" (Psalm 16:8–9 NLT).

We packed both of my parents' cars with suitcases and supplies, almost as if I were going to college again. I had both yellow and green sheets, posters for the walls, photos to display, plastic bins filled with cleaning supplies, a cozy bathroom rug, and as many things as I could find to make my future room feel like home. Denise had even given me a Willow Tree Angel that played "O Du Frohliche," a German song I heard most often around Christmastime. The song made my heart ache for Austria and cry at the thoughtfulness of my friend.

This time I wasn't going to college, or Chicago, or Colorado, or Vienna, or any of the places I loved. I was headed to the hospital. For four weeks. The car was full, but my heart felt empty, like all it held was loss. I wasn't sure what I was even looking forward to, except the possibility that I may see Jesus really soon if this took my life.

Another good-bye. Good-bye, at least for a time, to the freedoms I so often take for granted: brushing my hair, running, swimming, and enjoying the sunshine, close friends, and especially hugs. Germs are everywhere, and they would soon be my ultimate enemy, keeping me from things and especially from the people I love.

God, how do I pray through loss? How will I pray through a transplant? Our relationship right now doesn't feel like it used to. It's almost like You have put a blindfold on me, and while we tandem-ride, You reach one hand behind You to grab mine. You're whispering, "Trust Me, trust Me." And You're leading me down an unknown road. It feels scary.

Before leaving for the hospital, we pulled up in front of Tammy's house to stop by their Memorial Day party. My stomach churned as I thought about telling my friends a final good-bye.

I patted my head to make sure my bandana covered my freshly bald head. Without my hair, I couldn't hide. This final chemo round would cause my hair to fall out again, so a week before I would need to shave my head, I decided to dye my hair purple. My niece Khloe selected the color. I didn't want to go through the process of bleaching my hair first and then dyeing it, so I just used the purple on top of my natural brown hair.

I also didn't want to put my hairdresser Rachael through another emotional moment of shaving my head, so my brother, Kevin, had agreed to do it. My three-year-old niece watched as Kevin took his clippers to my hair. I wondered what was going through her mind. After Kevin completed the shave, my scalp looked much like an Easter egg with bright purple splotches. He jokingly suggested taking paint thinner to my scalp, but I opted to ask Tammy what she thought when I stopped by her house afterward.

Everything was in place for the transplant to begin. I even had a PICC line put in, so they would have two access lines for chemo and blood draws. I wasn't familiar with PICC lines, but Tammy was. I was required to clean (flush) the line twice a day, so for these two days before leaving I had visited her in the morning and evening for her assistance.

I entered her kitchen with a bandana on my head. Tammy's youngest son Josh watched ESPN in the next room as I started to explain my head-shaving experience.

"Umm, my head is a nice shade of purple," I stated.

As I pulled the bandana off, her eyes widened as her mouth stayed closed and her cheeks filled with air, almost as if the laughter she held would explode.

"Can you help me clean my head too?" I asked with a grin.

I tilted my head from different angles, so Tammy could get a full view of my purple-Easter-egg-looking scalp. Then she became a woman on a mission, hunting for something to scrub my head that wouldn't hurt too much.

Before I knew it, I was leaning over her kitchen sink while she took a toothbrush to my head with soap and water. Josh couldn't stay on the couch any longer. He had to come see what was causing all the laughter in the kitchen.

"Mom, what are you doing?" he asked.

"Trying to get the purple off of Miss Krishana's head," she giggled.

"Hey Josh, will you take a photo?" I knew this would need documentation. *God, thank You for this reminder to laugh. Laughter and tears, I can embrace both to get through this.*

SIGN ON THE DOTTED LINE

Weeks before Memorial Day, my body was still jet-lagged from packing up my Austrian apartment when I launched into a series of tests and appointments to make sure I was healthy enough to undergo deadly chemo.

I wanted every moment I had left before the transplant to be full of all of my favorite things: family, friends, good food, and memorable moments—especially while attending baseball games.

On the way to a Little League game, my phone rang. I knew that number. It was the transplant hospital. That number meant—no fun, all seriousness. I didn't answer.

The voicemail message appeared on my phone. As I listened to my transplant coordinator, I could feel my anger-level rising. The day to sign the final paperwork had been changed yet again. Tears pooled in my eyes. I wanted to throw my phone out of the car window. *Maybe if they can't reach me, they will go away,* I thought. My plans for fun, my last few moments outside of the hospital walls, were being disrupted again. I didn't feel like a person, only a future patient.

My mom and I made the trip to the transplant hospital and were escorted back to the same room where we had first met with the transplant doctor and coordinator. The doctor walked in with a stack of papers. Almost like a high-level college course, she outlined the procedures, risks and policies, and discussed the papers I'd need to sign.

This wasn't Longmont, Colorado. It wasn't Lauren's birthday, and I wasn't signing to put on a jumpsuit and goggles for the most amazing adrenaline thrill of my life. This jump was *not* for twelve minutes. This wasn't even simply a major surgery. The repercussions could be life-taking, life-altering, and life-long. I was signing up for more loss. Temporary loss such as losing my hair or my privacy. And other loss such as the possibility of never being able to have biological children.

My eyes strained as I attempted to focus and concentrate on all of the statistics, drug names, and very descriptive chemo side effects. I felt like I was in German class. My mind kept wandering.

I snapped back into the present moment as the coordinator handed me a pen.

God, do I really have to sign these papers? What about all of my dreams?

When we left the appointment, I decided I couldn't sit for an hour and a half while my mom drove. So I got in the driver's seat. Before pulling out of the parking lot, my mom looked at me with tears in her eyes and said, "I wouldn't have blamed you if you hadn't signed those papers."

"Thank you," I whispered.

The rain poured all the way home. Almost like navigating through God's tears.

ARRIVAL DAY

I hardly slept the night before our arrival at the transplant hospital. So I was thankful my first day only involved getting settled and taking in a lot of information.

God, this time with You is obviously gonna have to look different. Help me. You're in control of my body. If it be Your will would You wow the doctors, nurses, staff with how You work through my body? There are so many details they are "claiming" over me like blood transfusions, need for platelets, mouth sores, etc. But I know You have the power to take me through this and my experience not be what they typically see.

As I opened my Bible, I turned to Hebrews 5:7-8 NLT: "While Jesus was here on earth, he offered prayers and pleadings, with a loud cry and tears, to the one who could rescue him from death. And God heard his prayers because of his deep reverence for God. Even though Jesus was God's Son, he learned obedience from the things he suffered."

I wonder if that's how infants pray—with loud cries and tears. I already feel helpless, and they haven't even obliterated my immune system. I want to pray like that, completely dependent on You.

FROZEN

Within my first week in the hospital, the container with all of my furniture, dishes, and items from my Austrian apartment arrived at my Indiana residence. I couldn't help unload, supervise, or even be there in person. It was my first of five solid days of chemo. The countdown to what the stem-cell transplant team called Day 0, a new birthday, the day I would receive the brand new cancer-fighting cells after depleting whatever was left of my immune system. My final day of chemo involved a new drug. The nurses told me it could cause sores in my mouth a week later. The sores could become so bad that I may not feel like eating and the domino effect could continue. If I'm not eating, then my body isn't able to recover and help make my new cells at home in my body.

From past chemo experiences and what I had learned from my nurses, the best way to avoid mouth sores was having something frozen in your mouth before and while the chemo was administered.

"Good morning, Krishana. How are you, today?" Nurse Maggie asked as she walked in.

"Not too bad," I said with apprehension in my voice. "When should I start eating Popsicles?"

"You can start that in just a few minutes. Let me make sure everything is ready to begin the chemo," she replied and left the room. This would be the final punch to my immune system.

My room had both a small college-dorm type sofa bed and a hospital recliner. My dad sat upright in the recliner, ready to begin the Popsicle regimen. I had instructed him to keep walking back and forth to the kitchen to bring me Popsicles until I said stop.

Nurse Maggie gave me the signal to begin eating Popsicles. My dad was ready with my first one. Not too bad. Cold, orange flavored and actually refreshing. I made sure to cover every inch of my mouth with the cold, sweet goodness. *This might be the best chemo day yet,* I thought.

I guess I should've finished that thought with, *Says no one ever.*

Orange, cherry. "Dad, can you get me more Popsicles?"

Grape, lime. Maybe it was the sugar or maybe it was the nervousness, but my heart was pounding.

Cherry, grape, orange, lime. *I really don't want anymore. Don't give up, Krishana. Keep going.*

Lime, grape, orange, orange.

Twelve Popsicles in an hour.

But I wouldn't know until a week later if all of that Popsicle consumption had even helped.

Later that day, a brief tap on the door and a man in a white coat and bow tie walked in.

"I'm here to inform you that your cells are delayed," he proceeded to tell me.

"Delayed?" It's almost as if his words transported me back to the skydiving airplane and he had just pushed me out. *Wait, I didn't even get a 1, 2, 3,* I thought. *I didn't have time to anticipate.*

"Yes, they are coming from a long distance and won't make it to the hospital in time to begin the transplant tomorrow. We will implement the transplant on June 5."

"They got delayed in Chicago, right?" I chuckled.

His serious expression didn't change. "Well, we don't know their exact origin, but I'm sure transportation has something to do with it," he responded. I let him continue his job of informing me of this change and simply nodded my head. Then he walked out of the double doors.

Everyone was gone—my chemo was finished for the day, and my parents had left to have some time outside of the hospital. The "what ifs" started to congregate in my mind. A completely depleted immune system and cells that are late. Now I really felt empty.

God, You are never late. Talk about having to trust You in these moments. My life is in Your hands. Thank You for not letting go. Thank You for every moment. Thank You for Your strength pumping through me—for being my Sustainer.

He responded: "I will *be* your God throughout your lifetime—until your hair is white with age. I made you, and I will care for you. I will *carry* you along and *save* you" (Isaiah 46:4 NLT, emphasis added).

Something a friend had told me came to mind, "It's in that emptiness that hope is found. It sums up the gospel." Jesus came to be our hope in the middle of emptiness and loss and fear and uncertainty. And when stem cells don't show up on time. Hope has never left. He will be. He will carry. He will save me.

On the morning of June 5, Nurse Maggie entered to say that my cells had arrived. My mom returned that day with a birthday balloon and a pack of four cupcakes from a bakery back home. My stomach didn't feel like cupcakes. The chemo was working. My body was depleting. Even my appetite. But hope was on the way. Someone else's blood to give me a fresh life.

Nurse Maggie brought the cells into the room. She hung the bag on my IV pole. After connecting me to the bag of blood, she set the system to regulate transplanting the cells slowly. As the red trickled from the small plastic tubing into my body for five hours, I knew somehow on this ride, God saw what was ahead. A view I still hoped to see. "My purpose is to give them a rich and satisfying life" (John 10:10b NLT). I hoped I would be able to experience this fullness of life without the looming dark cloud of cancer.

CHAPTER 17

My Body Knows Better

I praise you because I am fearfully and wonderfully made; your works are wonderful,
I know that full well (Psalm 139:14).

Put me in the cage with the glass walls and watch me eat, drink, sleep (maybe), breathe, move. I felt like an animal at the zoo. I couldn't handle one more day on the third floor of that transplant center. I hungered for privacy.

The anti-rejection medicine that aided the new cells in making themselves at home in my body had to run through an IV pump twenty-four hours a day. I couldn't take a shower without being hooked to an IV pole. This involved a nurse coming to unhook me for a few seconds while I undressed and then to rehook me before getting in the shower, basically with one arm wrapped in plastic wrap and hanging out of the shower curtain. After the nurse left, the shower was the only place I could be alone. I could have those "on my knees" moments with God. I could cry and be and sit. This was my sacred place. So I took the longest showers.

I am Yours. Embrace me with Your hope and rest, Lord Jesus. This was a prayer

I had created from a handful of verses (Romans 5:5; Matthew 11:28-30; Colossians 3:12) that I had repeated enough that I didn't even have to exert energy to remember it. It played on a continuous loop in my being. I leaned my head against the shower wall allowing those words individually and collectively to saturate my heart.

I was so worn. *Yes, Lord Jesus, Embrace me with Your hope and rest. Both my physical body and my heart are tired. I don't know how to find rest here. It seems impossible. Help me.*

Daily walks and joking with nurses breathed some life and hope back into the turtle-pace of each day.

My dad and I walked to the other sections of the hospital most every day. When my white blood cell counts were too low (revealing my suppressed immune system), it depended on which nurse I had whether I was allowed to head as far as the parking garage. I had to promise I would wear a mask, take my IV pole, and thoroughly wash my hands when I returned. Since I went with my dad, I let him lead the way and touch every door handle and elevator button.

Those walks were slow as my body was depleted of everything, but there was a richness in those moments. Dad and I called our journey to the other side of the hospital, "visiting the swanky side." This part of the hospital had a modern feel with clean lines of interior décor, neutral tile flooring, a café with small, round black tables and black metal chairs, a Starbucks, and even a black grand piano. It was my own way of escaping the third floor transplant unit, which was mostly built of concrete with worn floors and gray walls in each room. I had covered all that gray in brightly colored signs of Bible verses and encouraging quotes.

One of my nurses, Ann, and I joked about conjuring up a plan so I could join her and her family on their beach vacation. Since the nurse tech came to check my vitals every four hours, if I put pillows in the bed and left right after the tech had come, potentially I would have four hours before anyone would realize I was missing. We still had to figure out how we would get my IV pole through airport security.

The nurses at the transplant hospital were constantly forewarning me about side effects. They kept telling me, "Well, next week you can expect mouth sores," or "Next week, prepare yourself for more fatigue and a fever." I was constantly on the watch for these dreaded symptoms. But God, holding me in His hands, somehow protected me from believing their words and taking them on as truth. He had something else in mind. He wanted to answer my prayer and wow them with His power. I came through without a fever, without mouth sores, and maintained movement by walking almost every day. Finally, the transplant team decided they wanted to unofficially make me their stem-cell transplant poster child.

I wasn't striving to push through a day like I used to do. There wasn't energy for a game-face. All I had was enough strength to trust Him for each moment. Even through the hardest moments, God left me reminders of His love and care.

One morning, a terrible migraine left me in so much pain that the only way my body could release the built up tension was to vomit. In between getting sick, I curled up into a ball in my bed, pulling my Bible in with me. I reached for my phone on the side table and quickly texted Tammy. "I need prayer. Now. Terrible migraine, throwing up."

She texted back, "On it."

God, help.

Eventually, the vomiting subsided, and I fell asleep. When I woke up, I had several texts and voicemails. So many people had been praying for me. Word got around so much that one of my friends who is a massage therapist dropped her afternoon schedule to drive almost two hours to help relieve the tension and stress in my body. The more I gave up trying to anticipate and, instead, allowed God to take the lead, the more I began to see Him reveal himself.

Early one morning a physician assistant came to check on me. She went through her tasks and asked me questions. As she headed out the door, she looked at me and said, "You hold onto that sign right there," as she pointed to a turquoise canvas that displayed Psalm 86:11, "Teach me your way, O Lord, and I will walk in your truth; give me an undivided heart, that I may fear your name." Even though I was isolated in a hospital, I was never alone. He was always with me, taking care of me.

God was in charge of the exact day they would allow me to go home, but it didn't change my constant prayer for that event. Going home meant freedom. And while I was unsure what it would be like at home, I knew it had to be more glorious than this.

FREEDOM!

The bump up the curb and into the driveway didn't feel as disruptive because I was distracted. A huge sign was planted in our front yard: "Welcome Home." The bright colors warmed me from within and triggered my cheeks to draw into a grin. Welcome. Home. A new invitation. A new season. The hardest part was over. I had made it. Now I could get on with my life.

The goal was to make it to 100 days past my transplant without acquiring graft versus host disease (when the new cells don't make themselves at home and start wreaking havoc on your health).

With each day I was home, I reveled in the freedom I had. I could decide when I wanted to eat and was thankful it didn't involve hospital food. It felt so good to walk around the house without an IV pole. The more I walked around, the stronger I got. And eight hours of solid sleep looked great on me. I was even finally able to take my anti-rejection medicine by mouth.

My parents had designated three rooms in the house specifically for me. I needed a space outside of my bedroom and bathroom to relax and be out of bed. I couldn't stop expressing to anyone around me how much I enjoyed being out of the hospital.

Days after being discharged, I had even convinced Tammy to take me to my favorite Mexican restaurant. She agreed as long as she wiped down the entire booth with Clorox wipes, I wore a mask, brought my own bottled water to drink, and I didn't tell anyone. I couldn't have chips and salsa, but just being at a restaurant felt like an adventure.

I needed to be daring, well as daring as I could be in my condition. I started to journal and began to dream again. These weren't Austria-size dreams yet. These were a bit smaller: Who would I spend time with next? How could I creatively use this time when I wasn't allowed to have a full-time job? I even contacted my German tutor, Barbara, and she agreed to continue our language learning sessions through Skype.

How could I invest in the relationships I had right here? Was there even a possibility that I could still mentor teen girls through my church—even if it did have to involve a mask and thoroughly washing my hands? As I regained strength, opportunities to pick up pieces of a normal life felt limitless. They felt good.

Good morning God! Thank You for the rain. Rain, coffee, the Word, Your Presence—aww! I could just drink it all in. I'm just thinking about how I really don't like going to the doctor at all, but back in February 2010, You urged me to make an appointment to see what was going on with my body. I trust that You will show me, and urge me to take the necessary steps to get treated. Thank You that Your Spirit is continuing to change and renew me daily.

He responded: "May our Lord Jesus Christ himself and God our Father, who loved us and by his grace gave us eternal encouragement and good hope, encourage your hearts and strengthen you in every good deed and word" (2 Thessalonians 2:16–17).

Thank You for Your encouragement. Thank You that we still journey together.

DO I LOOK SICK?

It was mid-afternoon. I was sitting in my recliner when my phone rang. I recognized the number. The transplant hospital. My heart started to beat faster remembering every time my coordinator would call before my transplant and I'd need to rearrange my schedule for an appointment. My blood counts (white cell, neutrophils, hemoglobin, platelets, etc.) had decreased some that past week, and I had been going to get Neupogen shots every day for the last six days. I wondered if this was what they were calling about.

"Hello?" I answered.

"Hello, is this Krishana Kraft?"

"Yes, ma'am, it is."

"We received test results from your recent blood work, and it appears you have the HHV-6 virus."

My eyes stared up toward the ceiling. *How could I have a virus? I feel fine. I even went to a Little League baseball game last night,* I thought.

"OK," I responded hesitantly.

"We need you to come today to receive treatment for this virus. It is an urgent situation. We tried to find a place closer to you, but it doesn't seem that the hospitals there have it available. We realize you are a couple of hours away, so we can give you an after-hours appointment in our infusion center across from the transplant building. Are you ready to take down these instructions?" the nurse asked.

I tore a page out of my journal to write the instructions. The word *urgent* blared in my mind. I knew I needed to move out of the recliner and toward my parents' room to tell my mom what was going on. My body didn't want to move. I didn't want to go. I wanted to go back to the moments before the phone call.

Mom and I arrived at the infusion center where I had been instructed to go. Hardly anyone was there.

The medicine hadn't arrived.

The insurance hadn't paid for all of it yet.

And the nurse wasn't familiar with administering it.

The *urgent* word blared again in my head. After all I had been through, I couldn't give up now. This medicine typically took three and a half hours to be administered, but since I was at the infusion center, they decided to speed it up since I seemed to be OK.

I distracted myself with the book I brought. I didn't need to think about nausea or throwing up. This wasn't my normal chemo days. This would help get rid of the virus. The virus I didn't even know I had.

Hours later, I was in the car, holding onto the inside of the car door. My stomach didn't like this medicine, and I couldn't hold it in. They said it wasn't supposed to make me sick, but it did. I threw up most of the way home.

When my stomach settled, it was time for a pity party. I wanted to throw all of the medicine they had packed in my trunk in the trash. Once again, my freedom was gone.

Three-and-a-half hours twice each day every twelve hours. They had taught me how to work the IV pump and administer the medicine myself. That was seven hours of my time connected to an IV pole. Seven hours at home. Seven hours away from being at baseball games, with friends, enjoying life, away from everything that breathed life into my soul. *Why, God, why? I don't understand,* I thought.

My life felt like a frayed rope. Each incident pulled away a bit more of the thickness and strength the rope once had. I was worn. I wasn't sure how much longer I could do this.

THE WHITE FLAG

After two weeks of treatment, the nausea wasn't getting any better, even with anti-nausea medications. I continued to throw up after administering the medication. My blood work continued to show the virus, and the latest plan was to continue to take the medication for at least six weeks.

This cannot go on for six weeks, I thought. I was barely eating anything. Something had to change, so I called my local connection to the transplant hospital, Sandy. She coordinated local post-transplant appointments for me with Dr. J.

"Sandy, I can't do this anymore," I painfully exclaimed. *Surely, they would realize that something is really wrong. I wouldn't normally do something like this. This is my white flag of surrender.*

"Krishana, let me make some phone calls, but go on and head to the hospital here in town," she responded.

My mom and I were fifteen minutes away from the hospital when the transplant hospital number appeared on my phone.

I answered.

"Krishana, we would like you to come *here* so we can monitor everything."

"But we're almost to the hospital! Do you realize that I'm not feeling well? We don't have any of our belongings," I said.

"We would like you to be here as soon as possible. We'll have a room waiting for you," the nurse said.

I took down the information and asked my mom if she wanted to go home to pack a bag or drive toward the transplant hospital. We decided to drive.

I can't believe this is happening, I thought. Heading back to the transplant hospital meant being back on the third floor of the stem-cell transplant unit.

Two hours later, Mom and I pulled into the parking lot of the transplant center. The nurses standing around the nurses station looked at me surprised.

"We didn't know you were stopping by," Nurse Maggie exclaimed, as if she was delighted I would come by to say hello.

"I'm actually not stopping by," I said. "I'm supposed to be admitted. They told me you would have a room for me."

The nurses looked at each other. No one knew I was coming.

They led me to a recently remodeled room. The only problem was that the bed hadn't been returned to the room. I couldn't stand up any longer, so I sat on the small sofa bed next to the window.

Person after person in a white coat came to ask me about my symptoms and why I was being admitted. The questions were making me more nauseous. Finally, two servicemen rolled in a bed. That was the most relieving thing anyone had done that day.

The questions continued and so did the vomiting. The anti-nausea medications increased. I went from one drug to keep me from puking to four drugs. One of them caused my eyes to be heavy and my vision blurry. I would try to look at my phone with one eye opened and the other eye closed. But I didn't make much sense anymore, in what I said or in what I was texting to friends. And I continued to throw up the medication to treat the virus. I couldn't keep it down.

TRUE CONVERSATIONS

I had been at the transplant center for a week. It seemed like only hours, considering I was either throwing up or so drugged that I was in a sleeping-state. My parents had both taken turns spending the night with me, even my brother had come to stay one night. Every time I'd turn on a movie or a show for us to enjoy together, I was asleep within minutes.

I knew I was messed up, but I wasn't sure what to do about it.

My Bible had a place in my hospital bed under the covers. So close, I snuggled up next to it. God was near. He promised never to leave me. He was the only One who truly understood what I wanted to say and scream and do. He knew every detail of what was happening inside of my body. I imagine conversations with Him were the only ones that made sense.

Be near me, Father.

I AM. "Be strong and courageous. Do not be afraid or terrified because of them, for the LORD your God goes with you; he will never leave you nor forsake you" (Deuteronomy 31:6).

I don't understand.

I get it. I understand that you don't understand. "Have you never heard? Have you never understood? The LORD is the everlasting God, the Creator of all the earth. He never grows weak or weary. No one can measure the depths of his understanding" (Isaiah 40:28 NLT).

Help me stop throwing up.

Krishana, you don't understand, but this needs to happen. "Jesus replied, 'You don't understand now what I am doing, but someday you will'" (John 13:7 NLT).

I want to be well.

I want that for you too. "The thief's purpose is to steal and kill and destroy. My purpose is to give them a rich and satisfying life" (John 10:10 NLT).

I don't want to be here anymore.

I AM home. I AM with you. You're with Me. "God is our refuge and strength, always ready to help in times of trouble" (Psalm 46:1 NLT).

THIS ISN'T WORKING

I don't remember the conversation about Tammy coming to visit, but my eyes lit up when she walked into my hospital room. She stood at the door and waved at me. She was trying to read me; I could see it in her eyes. Somehow she knew I wasn't myself.

She had come to give my parents a break. That evening she got out supplies to give me a pedicure. I sat in the room's recliner, and she soaked my feet and painted my toes. As she painted, I could barely keep my eyes open. The anti-nausea medicine was taking me toward my unconscious sleeping-state. Having no concept of how long I had been waiting for my toes to dry, I started to get up.

"I need to lie down," I said.

"OK!" she hurried around frantically pulling back blankets and preparing the bed and my toes so I wouldn't get nail polish everywhere. She helped me get into bed with my toes uncovered and the vomit-bucket beside me.

The next day, one of the transplant doctors came in to talk with us about the virus. My recent blood work came back. The virus was replicating. This didn't make any sense.

God, am I dying? Is this it? What if this virus doesn't go away?

I was scared. I looked at Tammy sitting on the sofa beside my hospital bed.

"Are you scared?" I asked.

"No, I'm angry!" she responded.

I was confused. In some ways, I was angry too, but it was stuck inside of me as if someone had tied me up and put duct tape on my mouth. It was caught in my throat. I couldn't get it out. This regimen wasn't working. This medicine needed to stop. *Was this killing me?* I thought.

"Krishana, why do you keep taking medication that isn't working?" Tammy asked.

This wasn't a trick question. I should have an answer and an opinion and a voice, but something held me captive.

"I don't know," I responded with exasperation. I wanted to cry. I didn't understand why I couldn't say no when I so deeply wanted to.

Tammy continued to ask many questions on my behalf, sometimes when the doctors, nurses, or staff didn't want her to. When my parents returned, she brought them up to speed and urged them to stop the medication. The whole situation was strange. Why would the medication that was supposed to be helping me get rid of this virus only cause it to increase? Tammy hesitantly headed back home, while my mom took over the next shift.

The next morning one of the transplant doctors on the team who hadn't been closely associated with my medical treatment took a curiosity in my case. She came in and sat down with my mom and me.

"I'm trying to think out of the box," she said. "Could either of you tell me what Krishana was like before she started to take this medication?"

"They called her the poster child for stem-cell transplants," Mom said. "She was walking outside and attending baseball games, making sure her skin was completely covered to protect her from the sun. She didn't overdo it but conserved her energy for the things she loved. She vomited a few times after chemo or when she had a migraine while she was in the hospital for her transplant, but after returning home, her appetite increased and the vomiting had stopped."

The transplant doctor took notes as my mom talked.

"As I've researched this virus, it seems there could be the possibility that this virus is actually dormant in your body rather than active. It shows up in your blood work because it is there, but it isn't causing any harm. This is similar to how the chicken pox virus remains in your body long after you have actively had the virus," the transplant doctor explained. "I will discuss this with your transplant doctor, and we will stop this medication."

Finally an answer or at least someone who was thinking outside of the norms for the situation. If this was a dormant virus, then throwing up the medication made sense. I didn't need it.

Once Tammy heard the good news, she texted me, "They could put you on all the anti-nausea drugs in the world, but your body knew it didn't need that medication because you're fearfully and wonderfully made. God knew all along!"

Three days later, I held onto the inside of the car door as we drove back home. It felt wonderful to be home. Even the carpet felt good under my toes. I had weaned myself off of three of the four anti-nausea medications but found myself quite altered.

As I sat on the floor in the extra bedroom where I had my recliner, my mom came to the doorway.

"Krishana, what would you like to eat?" she asked.

I looked at her. I knew she had asked me a question. But what was the question? And what is the answer?

"Would you like something to eat?" she gently repeated.

Finally, after a couple of minutes, I responded "No thank you." The delay in my response scared me. Why did I have so much trouble responding to a simple question? I decided to unwind with a hot bath.

As I sat in the tub, I sobbed. *God, why am I so messed up? Why do I have to start this healing process all over again?* The tears dropped one by one in the bath water. I knew He heard me, but I wanted Him to change things now.

CHAPTER 18

Come to the Mat

"I have loved you with an everlasting love; I have drawn you with unfailing kindness.

I will build you up again..." (Jeremiah 31:3–4a).

"I just want to punch something!" I said at breakfast with my friends Angela and Sidra. "I keep wondering where I would be health-wise if this had never happened."

I was beginning a new year and heading toward my one-year re-birthday after the transplant. My memory was better, and my response time had quickened. Once my body was off all the anti-nausea medication, it took over and knew what to do. I vomited a few more times after returning home, the remainder from the forty-two doses of medication I didn't need. Eventually my appetite returned, and I had regained energy and strength.

At every turn, though, it seemed my body wasn't making the milestones I wanted it to. I had been the poster child of stem-cell transplants and then a mistaken diagnosis left me clamoring for hope among low blood cell counts and a PET scan that revealed questionable spots.

The middle-of-the-night sobbing had continued off and on for five weeks. As those closest to me asked about my mistaken-virus story, the pressure built and built. The tears started to trickle and then they got stronger, like someone had just pulled a kink out of a garden hose.

In the darkness of my bedroom, when it was just the two of us—God and me—He took me to those painful places—holding my hand.

Angela and Sidra looked at me with wide eyes for a few seconds. Then Angela broke the silence. "I have a heavy-weight bag and boxing gloves in my garage. No one is using them. Would you be interested in something like that?"

"Yes!" I exclaimed. "Wow, that would be incredible—to physically punch something instead of punching someone."

We laughed as we imagined me actually punching someone. But God knew there was a little more kicking and screaming in me than others could see.

Angela's husband, Joel, carried the boxing bag down to the unfinished basement.

"Where would you like it?" he asked.

"Right there will be fine," I said pointing to a six-by-six-foot area in between what was being stored from my Vienna apartment—storage tubs on one side full of dishes and books and pictures, and then my dining room table and chairs, sofa, desk, and other furniture on the opposite side. A week later, my dad and I poured sand into the base of the free-standing boxing bag to hold it in place.

As I put on the red boxing gloves, I stared at the bins and furniture that had created this boxing ring. Here I was surrounded by all the things that once made up my life in Vienna. It made me sad. It made me angry.

This time I wasn't sobbing; I was raising my fists toward God.

Why did You let this happen?

Right punch.

What happened to doing "immeasurably more than I could ask or imagine" (Ephesians 3:20)?

Left punch.

Why didn't You stop them?

Side kick.

Why am I not living in Austria right now?

Side kick.

This had been the plan all along, God!

Right punch. Left punch.

I don't understand!

Right. Left. Right. Left.

I only ever wanted to follow You!

Side kick. Side kick.

I only ever thought I was following You!

Side kick.

Why am I here?

Right punch. Left punch.

Why didn't I see that red flag when the insurance didn't comply right away in giving me that virus medication?

Right. Left. Right. Left. Right. Left.

Why didn't I ask more questions?!

I punched and punched and punched. Then I crumpled onto the yoga mat next to me. The garden hose had been turned on again.

The anger and unforgiveness was not just toward the transplant hospital and the team there. It wasn't just directed toward God and wondering where He was in these painful moments. I was angry at myself, thinking I had a way of stopping this scenario. Thinking I had missed the red-flag moments of decision and my lack of perfection had caused my body to be beaten from the inside-out.

As I sat on the mat, I whispered to God, "Where do we go from here?"

I was finally willing to sit with Him in the pain.

I hadn't been willing to sit in the pain with those around me. My suppressed immune system had forced me for a time to keep my distance from the public. I tried to be faithful in avoiding germs as much as possible and even gave up hugs for almost five months.

I used the no-hugs as a way to build walls, shutting everyone out. *Why should I share my pain with them? They can't even be near me.*

"The thought of my suffering and homelessness is bitter beyond words. I will never forget this awful time, as I grieve over my loss" (Lamentations 3:19–20 NLT). As more of my life had been taken from me, from hairs on my head to dreams of living in Austria, I reevaluated my identity and purpose. Before, Krishana had been the associate editor at *Brio*, the one who had a heart for missions, the woman with a sense of humor, the one who loved Austria. All of that doing and performing: my job, my adventures overseas, my goals, my German learning—all of that had become my identity.

My attempts of rebuilding myself didn't work. It only had me tangled and trapped. I needed help.

As the darkness of cancer began to blend with the light of a new season, I still found myself frustrated. I couldn't seem to catch up with how everyone else's lives had moved forward. No longer living in Austria, I felt the pressure of the American dream weighing on my shoulders. Where was the job, the husband, the two kids and a dog I was supposed to have at this point in my life at thirty-five?

In the middle of those dark places, God responded. I sensed He was saying: *Krishana, I delight that you joined Me here. Your authenticity before Me is beautiful. My daughter, this is deep relationship with Me—unloading your pain, your rage, your struggles, who you think you are and all that has happened. Release it. That would be a heavy load to continue to carry on our journey ahead. I want you to be free. I want you to* be. *You are My daughter of hopeful purpose.*

"Yet I still dare to hope when I remember this: The faithful love of the LORD never ends! His mercies never cease. Great is his faithfulness; his mercies begin afresh each morning. I say to myself, 'The LORD is my inheritance; therefore, I will hope in him!'" (Lamentations 3:21-24 NLT).

He was both in the pain and in the needed celebration. I was still alive 365 days after the transplant.

DIFFERENT DAYS, DIFFERENT RIDES

I imagine my adrenal gland held up a picketing sign that stated, "No more crises, without more pay!" after seven years of off-and-on wow-factor and crises—leaving my stable job, cancer, moving to Austria, cancer relapse, a stem-cell transplant and a mistaken virus.

I was afraid to take a step toward anything I desired, worried that at any moment the bridge of dreams underneath me would crumble. I became so afraid that I created moments of conflict with those I was closest to just so I could say, "See, there it is again. It seems that getting what I want will never be true." At least I'd be achieving something—a self-fulfilling prophecy. I didn't want life to slam the door in my face one more time. I wanted to anticipate it and be ready.

In fact, I wanted to pick up the old life I had before cancer and run with it. But those backpacks of my old life were way too heavy. They were like the ones I traveled with in Europe. They exhausted me just looking at them. I was different. God wanted me to take something from the season I'd been through, but it wasn't those backpacks. He wanted me to just *be*. He wanted me to recognize that a deep relationship with Him didn't flow from performance and doing more; it flowed from simply staying connected, trusting Him with every part of me.

Being felt so itchy. It was uncomfortable—like the tag inside of a new shirt that constantly rubbed the back of my neck. And I didn't understand what being had to do with dreaming. All of my dreams were tied up in doing. How can being *be* enough? What happened to doing and production and lists and goals?

Would I dare to dream? How did this dreaming and being come together?

All of the crises left me not knowing how to function in the ordinary. I didn't know how to value the everyday moments with God, the tandem-bike ride, and remember that He was just as much present in those as He was in the thrilling or scary, the tandem-jumps. I didn't need to keep hunting for the next tandem-jump. He also had adventure for me in the daily ride.

But I wanted to be back in that blue jumpsuit and goggles waiting for that moment when I could hear the 1, 2, 3 and throw myself into the wind.

I imagine God grinned as I walked around in that jumpsuit and goggles. *My daughter, I didn't call you to jump out of planes every day.*

Well, I wasn't necessarily ready to jump *out of* a plane, but I wanted to jump *on a* plane and travel back to Austria. Dreams of those familiar faces, imagining myself riding the U-bahn, missing how my legs felt to walk everywhere around the city.

The cancer fog was lifting, and I wondered how I ended up here. Maybe my new cells felt the same way. Southern Indiana was where I was from, but somehow it wasn't home anymore. God had tattooed Austria on my heart.

I'VE BEEN WAITING FOR YOU

A few months later, I headed out to a prayer and ministry center about forty-five minutes from my house. As I pulled into the long gravel driveway, I walked toward the main building, a horse barn with a green roof that had been converted into a place for prayer and worship.

I held both nervousness and excitement as I parked my car and walked inside. Jessica, a high school friend, had encouraged me to come. A group of volunteers often took time to pray for individuals, not only about circumstances, but also about their journey with God.

I knew some of the people who would be there. Tony, one of the men who was there to pray for me, his wife had been my high school small group leader. I had known their family for a long time. Their oldest child was a cancer survivor.

"Krishana, as I prayed for you, the first picture that came to my mind was an actual picture of you [from one of your] postcards of you with the tandem bike,"

Tony started explaining.

That was seven years ago. I used those photos on prayer cards I sent to mission supporters. Even after all of this time, I still found those postcards hidden in different boxes or folders.

Tony continued, "There is a sense of you not riding alone...a picture of the Lord, so faithful, showing up every day to ride with you. It's almost like it's a picture of a faithful husband to you. You've been able to ride through the hills with Him. Yet, even when you couldn't pedal, He was still there."

I was glued to his words. This was a love story.

"When you weren't able to pedal, He'd make stops along the path, to polish and tune up the bike. Preparing the bike expectantly, almost as if He was saying, 'That day is coming, I'm going to get it ready.'"

Tony's voice shook as he tried to choke back tears. I bit my bottom lip to keep it from quivering. His words spoke of a deep, intimate relationship with Jesus. His words reminded me of that couple on the bike, every Sunday riding through the hills.

"It was almost like the Lord was a sweet little old man, so patiently waiting for you. Him saying, 'I can't wait to ride with her again.' Almost as if He reflected a patience that you sometimes see with people who have been married and have loved each other a long time. Their heart is so good for their spouse, for the person whom they love."

My eyes trickled.

"God's still riding with you, Krishana. He's never stopped riding with you."

CHAPTER 19

An Invitation

"LORD, you alone are my inheritance, my cup of blessing. You guard all that is mine.
The land you have given me is a pleasant land. What a wonderful inheritance!
You will show me the way of life, granting me the joy of your presence and
the pleasures of living with you forever" (Psalm 16:5–6, 11 NLT).

I pulled up next to Tammy's car. Her kids were back in school now, but the warmth of the summer still hung on, so we walked in the park as often as we could. I felt lighter, not only physically because I had recently shed some extra pounds, but also because my schedule wasn't being controlled quite so much by oncology and post-transplant appointments. Yet stepping out with these brand new cells wasn't easy. I had to learn to trust God in a new way.

I wanted Him to move first and give me what I thought would make me secure. *Come on, God, give me that job, give me that security, give me at least a rug I can stand on and then I'll trust You again.* Again and again I'd go through job interviews, extensive interviews, and the door would close. Then I'd have to start all over—more time, more energy.

Um, God, we're not going anywhere? I didn't sign up for spinning class!

I wondered when I could get off this ride.

For years, I had pursued the dreams God had placed on my heart. I ran after those dreams because I was running after God. Running at an incredible pace, not concerned about the dangers that lingered around the bend. These were good dreams and desires, such as working for *Brio* and living overseas in Vienna and sharing Jesus with teens. Each dream had its ups and downs, but overall held incredible stories. Now I felt like I had nothing.

I wasn't even sure how to take these stories and create a résumé that would get me a job in the market that had changed during the six years I was pursuing or living overseas. Everything I had experienced felt irrelevant to what would seemingly move me forward as I began life again in the United States.

Throughout my cancer journey, I had come face to face with the stories of other women who were also battling cancer. Some of these precious women had husbands and families and incredible faith in Jesus and amazing ministries. Why did God take some of those women to heaven? Why didn't He take me to heaven? Wouldn't that have been easier?

I couldn't sort out in my heart God's reasoning, His Sovereignty, His big picture. None of it made sense to me. But He was calling me to an even deeper place—trusting Him and the number of days He had for me on this planet. Even though so often it was the last place I wanted to be.

"Why am I still here, Tammy?" I asked as we walked the paved path. This wasn't the first time I had expressed questions about my purpose. We kept walking, as she searched for the words to respond.

"Krishana, God still has you here on Earth for a reason: to bring Him glory. It's not for us to know how He numbers our days," she said.

I chewed on her words.

God, I can't be enough. You never intended me to be enough. Because You are more than enough. Yet, I've tried to take this new body out for a spin and some days it's great. And others, well....

I know You don't usually call me to something I'm completely qualified for—living in Austria, learning German, raising financial support, battling cancer, adjusting to a different culture, even writing and editing. You call me to something that You will equip me for—one moment at a time.

Living on Earth felt difficult; I had to keep going back to God. Otherwise all of these trials would seem like constant punishment. There had to be something important about the struggles. Somehow the struggles always brought me back to intimacy with Him.

Thank You that You understand, Jesus. I come to You desiring so much to just be. I have believed the lie that this life and even my relationship with You is completely about performance. I see You taking me into a new season. And so much of my old season has to go. You want me to kiss it good-bye.

He responded: Yes. This is all about *complete* dependence on Me—spiritual, mental, physical, emotional. "Now may the God of peace make you holy in every way, and may your whole spirit and soul and body be kept blameless until our Lord Jesus Christ comes again. God will make this happen, for he who calls you is faithful" (1 Thessalonians 5:23-24 NLT).

DOPPELGÄNGER

As I opened my email account, I noticed a strange name with the subject line "Happy Birthday" in my inbox. My birthday had been a month ago. At first glance, I assumed it was spam, but something intrigued me to open it and read more.

Today I found a thin letter from DKMS in my postbox. In this letter I read your name and your Adress. My way was much more easier than yours to the date of 4th (or 5th) of June 2013 and I'm very very happy that I can read about you now. I don't know what to tell you more than I thank to God that everything had worked. Greetings from Germany to Indiana.

This was my donor! It had been two years since my transplant, and I was finally finding out about the person who had given me his cells, so I could live.

Germany! God, You gave me a donor from a German-speaking country! The gift of stem cells with a ten out of ten match was incredible, but God went so far as lavishing me with His love through a donor many miles away. A donor whose location He knew would mean so much to me. I started to take screenshots of the email to send them to my family and friends. We had a name to go with the blood that dripped from that IV bag on June 5: Hendric.

Besides being delighted that my donor was from Germany, I loved all of the nuances in his email that I understood from German class, such as the reason why he spelled address with only one "d" or why he capitalized certain words that were nouns. With my German-English dictionary opened, I started to write back—in German.

As I typed, the tears fell. *God, if it hadn't been for these desires You had placed in my heart, I may have never taken German or been able to respond to Hendric in his heart language.* I knew my expression in German would be insufficient, but I hoped, as I had learned from my time in Vienna, that taking steps toward someone and their story is one of the greatest ways God could use me. I didn't have to be sufficient.

August 19, 2015

Hi Krishana,

I will try in English, I think it's a good idea practicing this language. I read your blog. Yesterday, I had to Google the word "popsicle" you dislike so much. Your writing style is quite good and in German "lustig" I like this style and it makes me laugh even in the middle of a "traurige [sad]" story.

And please no big thanks for a normal thing humans should do for each other.

I'm very grateful [Dankbar] that I can do such a work.

—Hendric

CHAPTER 20

Waiting for the Beautiful View

"He has made everything beautiful in its time. He has also set eternity in the human heart; yet no one can fathom what God has done from beginning to end" (Ecclesiastes 3:11).

I walked toward the Vienna baggage claim thinking about the euro coin in my pocket, ready to unlock the luggage cart. I had packed all of my personal belongings in one small carry-on but had two large duffel bags full of items for other people. One duffel had clothes and supplies for refugees in Vienna. The other was filled with goodies for the GEM missionary women, items only Americans living overseas would pay good money for, like canned pumpkin, green chiles and Reese's Peanut Butter Cups—little things that reminded them of their other home. It felt incredibly normal to be here.

I found my taxi ride to the suburbs of Vienna and headed toward Eric and Christy's apartment. I had heard about their new apartment. The building didn't exist the last time I was in Vienna, so it was a brand new addition to the neighborhood. These apartments were connected to an entire shopping center at the street-level.

When Christy told me they were moving close to where I used to live, it was hard to picture where that might be. However, their daughter Kati described it best during one of our Skype conversations.

"Krishana, remember when we would walk to the U-bahn station and you would tease me that in that field there were wild turkeys," Kati asked.

"Yes," I giggled.

"Well, we're calling our apartment Wild Turkey Manor!" she exclaimed with a smile.

I called Christy as we pulled up to the shopping center/apartment complex. She was in the shopping center picking up some groceries and would send Kati to help me into the apartment. I paid the driver and waited next to the entrance with all of my luggage. The wind was strong, but a wall close to the apartment building entrance blocked the intensity of the cold. As I peeked from behind the wall, I looked across the street at the Merkur grocery store. *I walked that parking lot almost every day,* I thought, *as I headed to catch the train to language school.* Only a block away was the apartment I lived in. I could feel the tears welling up in my throat. The wind whipped through my clothes once again, and as I stepped back toward the apartment entrance I heard my name.

"Krishana!"

I turned around in time to see a young teen girl bounding toward me. *Is that Kati?* I thought. She looked so much taller and more grown up than the little girl who would come spend the night in my apartment and want pancakes at 6 a.m.

"Kati!"

We both reached out our arms as we moved toward a big bear hug. As I gripped her tight, she whispered, "Krishana, I missed you so much."

"Oh Kati, I missed you too," I whispered back. I could feel the puddles in my eyes. I didn't want to let go, ever again—Kati or Austria. But I knew that this trip wasn't about my questions of whether I'd ever return to Austria. It was about *being* in the moments. This was part of the beautiful view.

SWEET RIDE

Barbara, my German language tutor had Skyped off and on with me since I had relocated back to the States. Sometimes for German lessons and other times just to talk. Through the years, Barbara kept up with my blog posts. We would joke how I needed to continue writing so she would have more to read.

We decided my return trip to Vienna needed to involve all of the things I loved there, such as coffee, the Christmas markets, and walking through the city. So we packed that all into one evening since a few of the Vienna Christmas markets had just opened. We walked the cobblestone streets perusing the sparkling ornaments. As we made our way to the top of the street, we found a shop with unique décor.

"Könnten wir reingehen [Could we go in]?" I asked.

"Ja, sicher!" she replied.

We walked around the store and came across a large metal calendar you could use year-round by affixing magnets to mark the month and date. At the top of the calendar was a picture of a tandem bike. Under the picture were the words: *Life's a Journey—Enjoy the Ride.*

"Barbara, schau [look]!" I exclaimed.

Barbara walked toward me. "Oh, das Tandemfahrrad," she responded. "Ich möchte dir den Kalender gerne schenken [I would like to give this calendar to you.]"

"Wirklich [Really]?" I asked, a bit stunned. "Dankeschön!"

God, I desire to be known for this type of living. Not just as a blog name, but as a lifestyle—a deep relationship and constant dependence on You.

IF THESE HALLS COULD SPEAK

I took the Straßenbahn to the other side of Vienna to the nineteenth district—the place Dawn and I first opened the door to Dr. T's office. I hoped he would be there, but I hadn't made an appointment.

I gripped the box of chocolates and pressed the button to signal the Straßenbahn operator that I wanted to get off at the next stop. I walked up to the door and looked at the panel of bright silver buttons. I pressed the one that said Dr. T and waited. No one answered. Finally, someone left the building, and I ran to catch the door before it slammed shut.

I stepped off the elevator and looked toward the office. Something wasn't right. The sign and logo of Dr. T's medical practice had been partially torn down. I could always try the hospital; sometimes he worked there in the evenings.

As I walked up the steps to the hospital entrance, my heart began to pound. I had to keep telling myself I wasn't there for chemo or a test or a scan. I was only visiting. Still holding tightly to the chocolates, I approached an older gentleman sitting behind a long counter. The moment he glanced my direction I began reciting what I had practiced in my head all the way there.

"Dr. T is already gone for the weekend," he responded in German.

I looked down at the chocolates, *Will I ever have the opportunity to say thank you?*

"Dankeschön," I responded.

I got on the Straßenbahn and used the forty-five minutes back to Eric and Christy's apartment to remind myself that I'm a woman who doesn't give up easily. So I sent a quick email to Dr. T letting him know I only had a few days in Vienna, my health was good, and I would like to see him before I returned to the States.

The next morning, I had a reply.

Dear Krishana,

What a great message. It would be the highlight of my year to see you. I'm sure we will find the time. Could you come by the hospital tomorrow?

Hope to see you soon!

—Dr. T

I climbed those hospital steps once again and walked toward the bright yellow footprints that were painted on the floor. I smiled as I thought about my time in Vienna getting chemo and my time in the United States. Neither experience would be one I'd want to relive, but both had helped me recognize there was strength in me, a God-given strength. The kind of strength that runs toward God and the strength of desire He places on my heart—including those of living in Austria even after battling cancer. This was also the kind of strength that helped me willingly hand all of these desires and dreams back to Him to take an unexpected road—a stem-cell transplant. Not knowing where the road would lead and wondering if it would be heaven, this road had curved around the edge of death.

The moment I saw him down the hallway, I burst into a greeting, "Hallo, Dr. T!"

"Krishana. Please come in," he motioned toward his office. "You didn't bring a friend with you. I thought you had so many friends in Vienna."

I laughed. "I still have many friends in Vienna, but I didn't bring a friend this time."

"Here, I have something for you." I handed him the chocolates and a card. "I want to thank you for everything you did to help me and organizing my treatment in Vienna."

Dr. T's face shifted as I expressed thanks. "I wish there had been more I could have done. It seems that your American oncologist had the right treatment plan in mind," he responded.

"Dr. T, there was no way we could have known what would happen. You did an excellent job in giving me the care I needed." I longed for him to really hear those words. I knew I needed those words just as much as he did. "Dr. T, you mentioned in your email that it would be the highlight of your year to see me. Did you have a difficult year?"

"Yes, there have been many difficulties this year. Krishana, you always have a smile, even when you had cancer you had a smile," Dr. T shared. "When you lived here you mentioned mentoring teens through a church you attended. Remind me, what church was that?"

"It's located in the twenty-second district." I responded, surprised at his question. "Could I show you the website?" pointing toward the computer on his desk.

"Please," he responded.

God, maybe You did more here than I even realize, not just in relationships with those living in Vienna, but even in my own heart.

GOD'S GOODNESS

Thomas, one of the church leaders, introduced me to the congregation. I stood before so many familiar faces—such as Jim and Waltraude and many others who had become a dear part of my world in such a short timeframe.

Many of those familiar faces knew my story. However, the congregation had grown and many didn't know me. I took the microphone and began to share my story.

"Even before moving to Vienna, my plans were interrupted, and I was diagnosed with cancer. This type of cancer was treatable but not curable. After four months of treatment, the cancer was gone. The desire to move to Vienna and serve God here was just as strong after that cancer diagnosis as it had been before."

Desire is good. It is powerful. It's God-given. Something about this desire to move to Austria and plant my life there had blossomed in the middle of horrific cancer. With each setback and as each desire was crushed, God pursued me. *OK, Krishana, hold My hand. We're going a bit deeper. You can trust Me, don't forget that.*

I cleared my throat and told the saga of cancer to remission to cancer again and the stem-cell transplant.

"These [stem] cells came from a donor in Germany. From a man named Hendric. I am thankful for his willingness to give such an amazing gift so I can live. Now, I have German in my blood. I'm hoping this will increase my ability to speak and understand German."

The congregation laughed.

I pointed to exactly where I stood on that stage: "…right here is God's goodness. I am here, in Vienna, Austria."

Standing there was another one of those beautiful-view moments. It was God's goodness that physically I could stand in front of this church. Yes, there were still so many questions that stirred in my heart, questions I may never understand the answers to. I took a deep breath as a tear streamed down my face. I was ready to continue. *God, I'm ready to move forward. Whatever that means.*

MORE?

I had already journeyed over steep heights of excitement and through valleys of disappointment and sorrow. Yet God was calling me to ride again. I couldn't imagine that He had anything else for me. But His invitation was to not give up hope and to believe that there was more.

I wanted to know what the "more" entailed. I used to think that meant a longer to-do list, high expectations, and performing well. I already held so much, so how could I hold any *more?*

As I continued to ride with God, I began to see this "more" wasn't about a new job or a new place to live or a new opportunity to jump. The "more" was God. I hadn't even scratched the surface in my relationship with Him and exploring who He is.

I could now see that with each loss, each disappointment, each tear, the tandem-living only grew sweeter. Our relationship grew through each setback. Even my anger and frustration in the middle of all the pain led me back to Him. The good things He had withheld had positioned me to receive *more* of Him—

because He was all I had.

This was only the beginning of my journey in understanding how God and His "more" had to do with freedom and very little to do with destination. He wants me to be free. When I live out of that identity, then it didn't matter whether I was in a blue jumpsuit, on a bike, or spending days in the hospital.

He was beckoning me to a deeper trust. Trust that He would show me not only which way to go, but also what to hold on to and let go of. Trust that He would reveal to me the junk in my life that we didn't need to take with us as we continued to ride. Trust that in *being* with Him I would be secure even when we were making incredible jumps and free falling or riding uphill, even blindfolded. And my only performance was trust. Trusting Him that this entire ride was leading toward a beautiful view.

God is the More. He's putting on the jumpsuit. He's polishing the tandem bike. He's ready, saying, "Will you join Me?"

Acknowledgements

Why can't I have at least 50 main characters? I wondered, as I prepared this story for the next steps in the editorial process. As I crafted scenes, I could see those people who brought meals after an all-day chemo treatment. I remembered the names of those who have been praying for me for years, some I have never met. I could see the family and friends as we Skyped while I lived in Austria. I pictured the familiar faces at the Evangelikale Gemeinde Kagran, Southeast Christian Church, the Center for Intercultural Training, and those at First United Methodist Church (Rutherfordton, N.C.) and Park Memorial United Methodist Church. I could see all of those who loaded and unloaded my container both in Vienna and in the United States. And the stories of how God provided even when I couldn't be there to help.

Beth, I could see you helping me paint my apartment wall in Vienna with many, many coats of paint. I could hear the treasured conversations over Wiener Melange at a Vienna cafe and the hilarious laughter when my family and friends did whatever they could to make me laugh (Mary Jo and her dancing skills) during hospital stays. I could hear the precious questions and rich prayers from children that still take my breath away. I could see all of the encouraging cards, the plethora of hats and the generosity. I could see the beautiful faces of many, many GEM missionaries and how our stories collided for a time and how I'm left changed. Before this was ever a story in a book, so many of you were a part of this real-life "ride." Thank you! Dankeschön! I'm forever grateful.

Hendric, I hope we get to meet someday, so I can hear your side of the story. But if not, know that I'm grateful for your willingness to be my stem-cell donor.

Kaleb and Khloe, thank you for being you! You are my favorites. Your Aunt Krishy loves you bunches.

Kevin, thank you for your immediate willingness to be my donor. Wow. While things don't always work out as we hope, I still see the ways you continue to love sacrificially, deeply and generously. I'm grateful to have you as my "little" brother. Thank you for loving me in those ways. I love you.

Mom and Dad, my words feel insufficient to describe how thankful I am for you. I lost count of the times you were right there when I needed you, especially those nights when I thought I might die with my head in a trashcan or on the bathroom floor because I was so sick. Thank you for also loving sacrificially, deeply and generously. Your Krishana Banana loves you more and more and more.

For those friends: Tammy, Kim, Diana, Laurie, Connie, Beth Ann, Tra'Cee, and Charissa who read the "early" versions of this book before I was even finished with the first draft, thank you for your encouragement along the way. Your words were life-giving even when the story-telling wasn't at its best. Thank you, thank you!

Andrea Vinley (Jewell) Converse, you're a brilliant editor. I'm grateful for all of your hard work and the ways you encouraged and challenged me in my writing and story-telling. This journey with you has been sweet.

Andrea Gutierrez, thank you for being the final set of "fresh eyes" before design. It's been a joy to work with you.

Lynn Wohland, your creativity and artistic talent still causes me to stop and be in awe. I love how God used you to create a drawing of "His Hands and the Pearl" years before I knew I'd have the privilege of working with you again on a book cover. Oh He is so good!! Thank you for being a part of creating the cover art for this project. I wouldn't have wanted to brainstorm and giggle with any other artist.

Sally Dunn, thanks for taking those tandem bike pictures many moons ago. Who would've thought we'd work together on a book. What a joy! Thank you! Only God could orchestrate something like that.

Dawn S., there is no doubt in my mind that our conversations were guided by the Holy Spirit. God is good to have brought you into my life at the perfect time. I'm not sure I would have been able to go to the places I've gone or even attempted to write about these places without your encouragement, challenge and support. Thank you for your constant reminder that my story is for me and brings glory to God. Thank you for sharing a bit of your Dawn-ness with me. I'm honored. You have taught me much and have so willingly and graciously walked with me. It was a joy to "paint" with you!

Troy and Beth Ann, I can't help but think of that night at a seafood restaurant in Washington State. Our conversation led me to believe I couldn't stand still in this any longer. I needed to take the next steps in writing this story and see how God would lead. Thank you for your friendship and encouragement along the way.

O Love, thank You, my God, for being alive in me. You are far more than my words will ever express, and I wouldn't want to have You in any other way. Thank You for tandem jumps and tandem rides, laughter and tears, adventures and adversity, fear and faith, pain and passion —and how embracing these has led to greater intimacy with You. Thank You that our adventures continue, and this is only the beginning. Thank You for the promise of an eternal beautiful view and that You are the More I've been searching for. Thank You for the blood that was sacrificed for me through Jesus Christ. I love You.

Discussion Questions

Use these as a jumping-off point and see where the conversation leads or even create conversation-starters of your own.

Introduction

1. Looking back at your life so far, describe a moment when you now see God pursuing you.

2. How have you been impacted by someone else and their journey with God?

3. What is it about God as Pursuer that excites you? Intimidates you? Frightens you? Comforts you?

4. If the tune God is singing over you right now had a name, what would that be in eight words or less?

Chapter 1

1. When have you told yourself, "I can hold this together, I can!"? Is there someone with whom you feel safe to share a piece of your story?

2. "I had to find a bridge to admit why I was really there, what I really needed." What holds us back from being honest when we're hurting? What types of "bridges" have you created in desiring to be authentic with someone else?

3. "It wasn't just about persevering or a performance, it was also about doing it in such a way that it couldn't fail. Being one step ahead of what might cause failure. Now, here I was face to face with my enemy—failure. And I couldn't perform my way out of this." Can you relate to this desire to be one step ahead of failure? How so?

Chapter 2

1. Share your "craziest-thing-I've-ever-done" story. What was the catalyst for this moment?

2. "I felt like I had just attended a pep rally for my heart. If I had known where to go or what to do next, I would've packed my cubicle immediately and headed out of town. God had my attention." When have you had a moment like that? How did God grab your attention?

3. What questions do the phrase "tandem living" with God spark?

Chapter 3

1. When have you felt your knowledge of God and "the next" He was leading you to not match up? How did that play out?

2. Which characteristic or attribute of God is like a worn blankey to you? Which is most uncomfortable?

3. Describe a time when you arrived at your next destination questioning if this was really where you were supposed to be. What did you do with that uncertainty? Did you question yourself, God, others?

Chapter 4

1. Are you more of a planner or more laid-back? How does your personality type impact your relationships?

2. Describe a time when you were lost. Who knew you were lost, if anyone? If you knew someone was looking for you, how did that impact you? If you knew no one was looking for you, how did that impact you?

3. When have you seen God use you to reach someone despite many obstacles?

Chapter 5

1. Share a time when you had to transition into a new location, season, job, etc. How did your past impact you? What was that transition like? What did you take with you from your past? What did you leave behind?

2. What's your typical self-prescription for anxiety?

3. *Jesus, what does it look like to move as You move? To go deeper with You?* Do you resonate with this prayer? Why or why not?

Chapter 6

1. *"God, did I hear You correctly?... You haven't asked me to push the tandem bike up the hill."* Have you experienced a time when what you believed to be the next step didn't add up with what was happening around you? Did you talk with God about that? What were those conversations like?

2. Share a time when humor broke the ice in a situation outside of your comfort zone.

3. " There wasn't time to pause—God's agenda was on the line. I knew He would be asking me to jump soon." Reflect on these sentences. What about these sentences do you resonate with? What don't you resonate with? What do these sentences say about what Krishana believed about God?

Chapter 7

1. "Biospy" was an unfamiliar, unknown and unbelievably scary term for Krishana. What do you do with a word like "biopsy"? Is there a word or moment for you when the unknowns felt bigger than the knowns? How did you respond to such a moment?

2. "I felt so helpless, so far beyond being in control. The only One I knew who really had any pull in this situation was the One who is always in control. I just thought He always needed my help." Were we ever in control? What reminds you of not being in control? How would a daily recognition of your frailty and not-in-control state change the way you lived?

3. "I stood by the kitchen table holding onto the closest chair. I swallowed hard. *God, this is worse than Dr. J imagined? Help me.* "Desperation prayers. When has "help" been the only word you could say out loud/pray? What did it feel like praying that? Where did the conversation with God go from there?

Chapter 8

1. From your perspective, what is the silliest thing you have ever prayed about? How do you weight prayers? Are there certain conversations with God that are more important than others?

2. When you're hurting, what is the best way someone could respond/reach out to you?

3. What feels more natural to you—laughter or tears? When have either/both of those been uncomfortable? Why?

Chapter 9

1. "Now, I had to relearn how to pedal-out this tandem living journey. My spiritual legs had become weak. My daily struggles and insecurities resurfaced as rough terrain on a bike path." Which parts of these statements do you resonate with? Why? Have you ever come through a difficult time realizing later how much God had "pedaled"? What caused this realization?

2. Who do you share your tears with? Why?

Chapter 10

1. When has God showed up at just the right time for you? How did it change the way you viewed Him? How did it change the way you approached Him after that incident?

2. How do sharing vulnerable stories create intimacy? What responses have you experienced after sharing a vulnerable story?

3. How could authenticity be an invitation?

Chapter 11

1. "The jump into Vienna had been breathtaking, but now I was pedaling with God along a steep uphill." Have you ever had a honeymoon-phase with God? What happened with your relationship when the "honeymoon" ended?

2. Krishana wanted to be one step ahead of whatever she could. When/where does this work? When/where doesn't this work?

3. How do you approach interruptions?

Chapter 12

1. What does it mean to stay within God's rhythm? What would that look like in your life?

2. When has taking a step outside your front door unexpectedly led to helping someone? What were your conversations with God like in those moments?

3. How have your life experiences increased or decreased your desire to walk alongside someone in a similar situation?

Chapter 13

1. "They do not fear bad news; they confidently trust the Lord to care for them. They are confident and fearless and can face their foes triumphantly" (Psalm 112:7-8 NLT). What's the difference between denying bad news and not fearing it?

2. Do you ever have trouble asking for help? If so, when? Why was asking for help difficult?

3. *"God, what are You doing? Why is this being taken away from me? All I ever wanted to do is follow You, and I'm here. Now I have to leave?"* When have you asked God what He is up to? What were those conversations like?

Chapter 14

1. Seemingly overnight, everything changed for Krishana from health to location to even occupation. What are practical steps you take to recalibrate during transition?

2. When have you said, "No one understands"?

3. "The only thing God was calling me to do was to trust Him with whatever the reasons and outcomes might be. He wasn't asking me to solve the mystery or connect the dots. I didn't need to know right then what the next few months held, much less the next few years." Are you a mystery-solver or a connect-the-dot kind of person? How does this impact your relationship with God? What does it look like to trust God with whatever His reasoning may be?

Chapter 15

1. When have you desired to pull the covers over your head in hopes that a difficult circumstance would simply go away?

2. Is God a part of your decision making? If so, how do you approach Him with those situations?

3. *"It feels as though there will never again be a beautiful view. All we're doing, God, is pedaling and pedaling. And this hill is steep. Where is this journey leading? How will You show up?'* '...I will never leave you nor forsake you,' (Joshua 1:5). I will not fail you, Krishana." How do you resonate with this prayer? What do you do with God's response? What impacts you the most?

Chapter 16

1. How do you embrace both laughter and tears?

2. *"I wonder if that's how infants pray—with loud cries and tears. I already feel helpless, and they haven't even obliterated my immune system. I want to pray like that, completely dependent on You."* How are your prayers infant-like or even child-like? How have your prayers changed to more of an adult-thinking? Contrast the two—how are they similar/how are they different?

3. When Krishana's cells didn't show up on time, there was no turning back. They had already obliterated her immune system. "Jesus came to be our hope in the middle of emptiness and loss and fear and uncertainty." Has this been true for you? If so, how?

Chapter 17

1. Do you and God have a sacred spot? If so, how have those locations changed in various seasons? If not, what would that look like for you today?

2. Have you ever had prayers that pray themselves? What would be the benefit of such a prayer? How could this connect to 1 Thessalonians 5:17?

3. When have you been in a situation where you didn't have a voice? What were your conversations with God like at that time?

Chapter 18

1. When have you raised your fists toward God? What did that scene look like? Sound like? Smell like? Feel like? Taste like?

2. Krishana used a suppressed immune system and a no-hug rule to shut people out of the pain she felt. How do you shut others out of the pain you're experiencing? How do you shut God out of that pain?

3. How do the trust and intimacy with God look the same/different when you compare the tandem jumps with the tandem bike ride? Do you consider one more valuable than the other? Why?

Chapter 19

1. When have you questioned God's purpose for your life?

2. Has God ever shown up in a way that was so personal to you, it overwhelmed you? How did that affect your relationship?

3. What does "be-ing" versus "do-ing" look like? Do you favor one over the other? Why?

Chapter 20

1. Describe a recent "beautiful view moment."

2. Have difficult circumstances ever revealed something about yourself you didn't know you had? If so, what was it? What did you do with it afterward?

3. How has this story moved you to explore God? How can you use your own story to explore God and to draw in other people?

4. "I could now see that with each loss, each disappointment, each tear, the tandem-living only grew sweeter. Our relationship grew through each setback. Even my anger and frustration in the middle of all the pain led me back to Him. The good things He had withheld had positioned me to receive more of Him—because He was all I had." Has your intimacy with God grown during difficult times? If so, how did it grow? What's the core of a relationship that grows through setback after setback?

5. What's your biggest take-away after reading *Tandem Living?*

About the Author

Krishana Kraft tends to find adventure in unexpected places. From a small town in southern Indiana, she holds a bachelor's degree in communications (journalism) and what feels like a master's degree in cancer. It's from those painful moments in her journey that led her to a deeper relationship with Jesus—an adventure unlike any other.

Formerly a *Brio* magazine associate editor (Focus on the Family) and missionary with Greater Europe Mission, Krishana continues to use her experiences to inspire and direct her position as a freelance writer and speaker. When not behind her Mac, she loves rich conversation, traveling around the globe, missions opportunities and inspiring young women toward intimacy with Jesus.

Join her on her adventures at **www.tandemliving.org**

LOOKING FOR A SPEAKER? Would you like Krishana to share about Tandem Living at your next event or retreat? Find out more about this opportunity at **tandemliving.org**.